PRACTICAL MACRAMÉ

EUGENE ANDES

All macramé articles pictured
are the work of Gene and Ellen Andes.

 STUDIO VISTA LIMITED / LONDON

 VAN NOSTRAND REINHOLD COMPANY / NEW YORK

Van Nostrand Reinhold Company Regional Offices:
New York Cincinnati Chicago Millbrae Dallas

Copyright © 1971 by Litton Educational Publishing, Inc.
Library of Congress Catalog Card Number 76–137499

Designed by Rosa Delia Vasquez
Type set by Brown Bros. Linotypers, Inc.
Color printed by Princeton Polychrome Press
Printed and bound by Halliday Lithograph Corporation

Published in New York by Van Nostrand Reinhold Company
450 West 33 Street, New York, N.Y. 10001
Published simultaneously in Canada by
Van Nostrand Reinhold Company Ltd.
Published in Great Britain by Studio Vista Limited
Blue Star House, Highgate Hill, London N19

SBN 289 701945
16 15 14 13 12 11 10 9 8 7 6 5 4 3 2

CONTENTS

Foreword   13

1	Materials 14	
2	The Basic Knots 20	
3	Using Leather in Macramé 36	
4	Two Simple Belts 40	
5	A Macramé Belt 44	
6	Fancy Macramé Belts 50	
7	A Macramé Hat 58	
8	A Macramé Purse 74	
9	A Hairy Purse 92	
10	A Macramé Bikini 96	
11	Macramé Vests (Waistcoats) 106	
12	Some Notes 116	

List of-Suppliers   118

Dedicated to the instructors in surgery who kept telling me all
that practice in tying knots would come in handy someday.
And to Jim, who told me when someday was.
And to Jac, who painted the bathroom orange.
But most of all to Ellen; it's her book.

With some help from his friends:
Larry Songy, color photography;
Lynn Franklin and Murph Dowouis,
black and white photography.

FOREWORD

This book is designed to help the beginner through a series of projects of increasing difficulty and sophistication, while decreasing his need for detailed instruction. Obviously, creativity cannot be taught. It is my aim, however, to get away from the approach to handwork which provides the beginner with a "kit" containing all the supplies and instructions needed to make something exactly like those produced by one thousand others who bought the same kit.

Macramé supplies are inexpensive, and the techniques learned from this book can be used to make other useful items.

1 MATERIALS

Cotton seine twine is the best material for most of the projects in this book. It looks good, dyes easily, and holds knots securely. It is the cord used by fishermen to tie nets and can be found in sporting goods or hardware stores catering to commercial fishermen. Ordinary seine is not at all expensive and is usually sold in one-pound hanks.

Cotton seine twine comes in soft, medium, and hard twists and is sized according to the number of threads in the twist. For vests and purses No. 36 to 54 medium or soft cord is suitable, and No. 72 to 90 medium is used for belts. The macramé bikinis pictured in Figures 16 and 17 are made with No. 18 to 24 medium or soft cord. The bikini requires about one pound of cord, with some left over for another project; and a vest (waistcoat) uses only about two pounds.

Unbleached cotton seine twine is nearly white, so you may want to dye it. If you do, be sure to wash it thoroughly so that dye will penetrate well. (Washing also removes any stiffening agents and softens the thread.) Coloring with commercial dyes is simple: divide a one-pound hank into three or more small, loosely wound coils, tie them lightly together so that dye will flow freely through the cords, and submerge them completely in a plastic or enamel pan of dye dissolved in the hottest water available (see Diagram 1). If none of the commercial shades please you, try mixing your own. I usually mix from three to five colors for my shades—for example, 1 part gold to ⅓ parts blue and brown makes a much nicer green than you can buy. Be sure when mixing your own colors that you dye enough cord to complete the project, because it's very hard to match colors once you run out.

1. Cord ready for dyeing

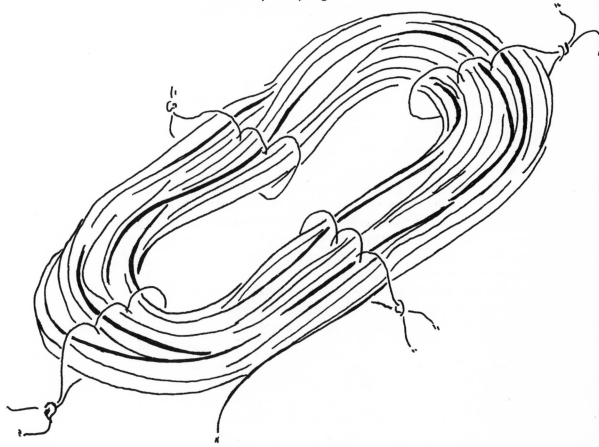

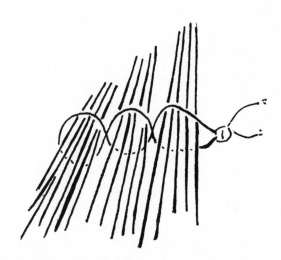

Note the way tie is interwoven to separate strands

15

Dark shades will probably have to be boiled to fix the color. Use the same amount of dye solution as for lighter shades and boil cord for about a half hour in an enamel pan.

Rinse dyed cord thoroughly to remove excess dye and dry it on thick pads of newspaper or on a clothesline. Remember that dyed cord is one or two shades lighter after rinsing, and lighter still once dried.

Follow the same procedure in dyeing a completed macramé project. If you wish to redye cord or a finished piece, it is wise to test the second dye on an extra piece of the original cord to be sure of the color. Articles with fringe are best dyed when finished, because unraveled fringe will show white where the dye has not penetrated to the inner cord.

Nylon cord is rapidly supplanting cotton for tying fishing nets because, unlike cotton, it does not rot. For macramé, however, it has several disadvantages: it is twice as expensive as cotton, dyes poorly, and tends to slip when knotted. Nylon takes dye less well than cotton, so boil the color in for about thirty minutes to get dark shades.

Many other kinds of cord or cordlike materials can be used in macramé projects. Among the most common substitutes are leather bootlaces, jute wrapping twine, and wool yarn.

Readying cord for tying   Before you begin a macramé piece, cut all the cord you will need into appropriate lengths. The easiest way to do this is to wrap cord around something half the desired length and cut it at one end. To illustrate: the vest in this book requires two pounds of twine cut into standard lengths of 14 feet. There are two doorknobs in my apartment, 7 feet apart, so I wrap the twine around the knobs and cut one end. In the absence of well-placed doorknobs, a pair of C-clamps and a table edge (see Diagram 2) or two chair backs work equally well.

In time you will be tying so rapidly that unraveling of the cord will not be a problem, but for now tie an overhand knot (see Diagram 3) in the ends of cotton cord as soon as it has been cut. With very long pieces, you can wind cord onto small bobbins or into balls and fasten with wire twists. If you're using nylon, melt the ends in a flame to fuse them. Be careful, because nylon is highly flammable. Plunge the melted ends in cold water before you touch them, or the hot nylon will burn your fingers badly.

Many projects call for a tying board. For larger ones, a piece of plywood measuring about ½ by 24 by 36 inches can be held comfortably in your lap or, if you prefer, leaned against the back of a chair like an easel. Belts are easily tied from a doorknob or hook or from your toe, and small items like purses can generally be done free hand. For bikini tops, I use my perfect size 34A knees as backing.

2.   This is a C-clamp

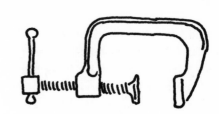

Distance between clamps is one-half the desired cord length

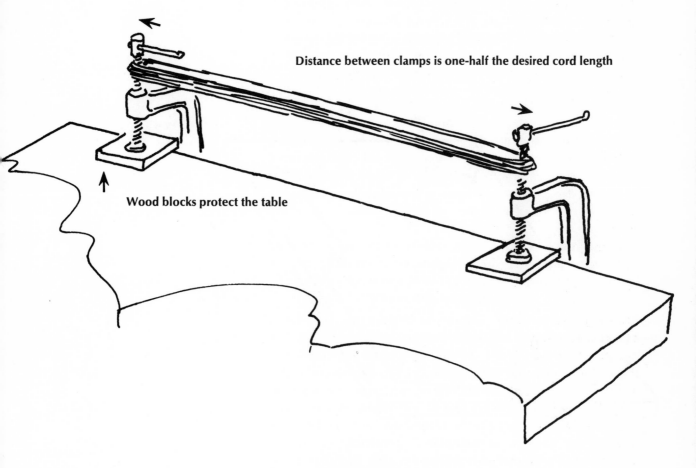

Wood blocks protect the table

3.   Overhand knot

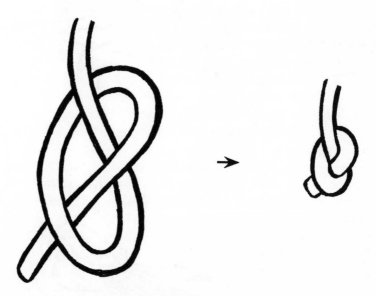

Small finishing nails or wire brads are used to outline the project on the tying board. One of the illustrations in Diagram 4 is a board arranged for tying a macramé vest. Note the two bent brads at the bottom, which are used as a cleat to fasten ends. A board can be used for several projects if you drive the nails in lightly so that they come out easily when you're through.

The only unusual tool I use in macramé is a hemostat clamp (see Diagram 5). This is a surgical instrument and is handy for pulling cord through holes in leather and beads (see Diagram 6). If you're going to buy one, get the smallest, or "mosquito," size.

4. Tying arrangements

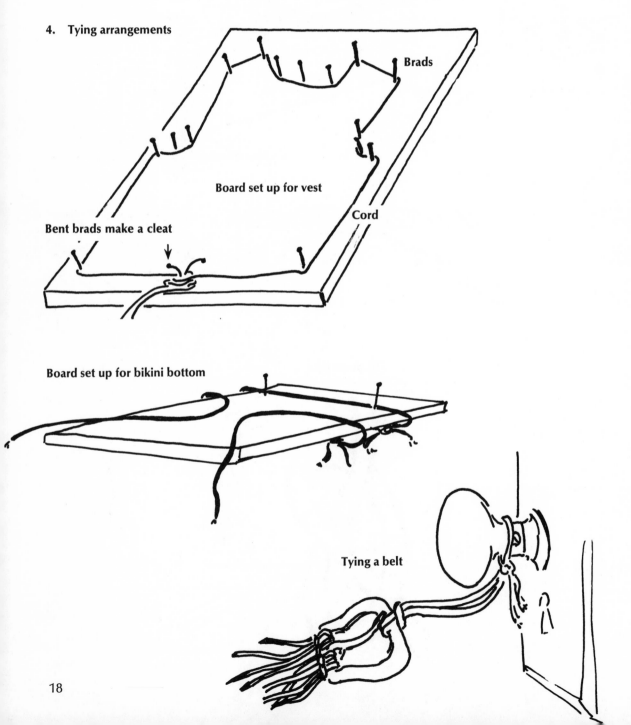

Brads

Board set up for vest

Cord

Bent brads make a cleat

Board set up for bikini bottom

Tying a belt

5. Hemostat

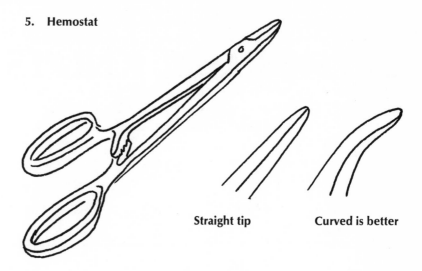

Straight tip   **Curved is better**

6. Wet cord. Twist around and pull through with hemostat

Use hemostat to thread cord through holes in leather

2 THE BASIC KNOTS

The half hitch, clove hitch, lark's head, and square knot are the basic knots in macramé. The complex patterns in this book are all merely combinations of these simple knots. The basic knots must be tied well and rapidly: Our first projects will provide you with ample practice for the more advanced projects.

The clove hitch and the lark's head knot are variations of the *half hitch* (see Diagram 7), a knot which is always tied over a supporting stick or carrier cord. As you can see, the half hitch can slip along both working and carrier cord, but if you tie a second half hitch you will produce a stable knot called the *clove hitch* (see Diagram 8 and Figure 1). The clove hitch is used most often in macramé when one cord crosses another. The clove hitch may be tied over a horizontal carrier as shown, or over a vertical cord. Either side of the knot may show on front of a piece. In many of the projects in this book, you will find that a clove hitch is followed by a half hitch as in Figure 2. This is an ornamental variation often used to cover a bare carrier cord.

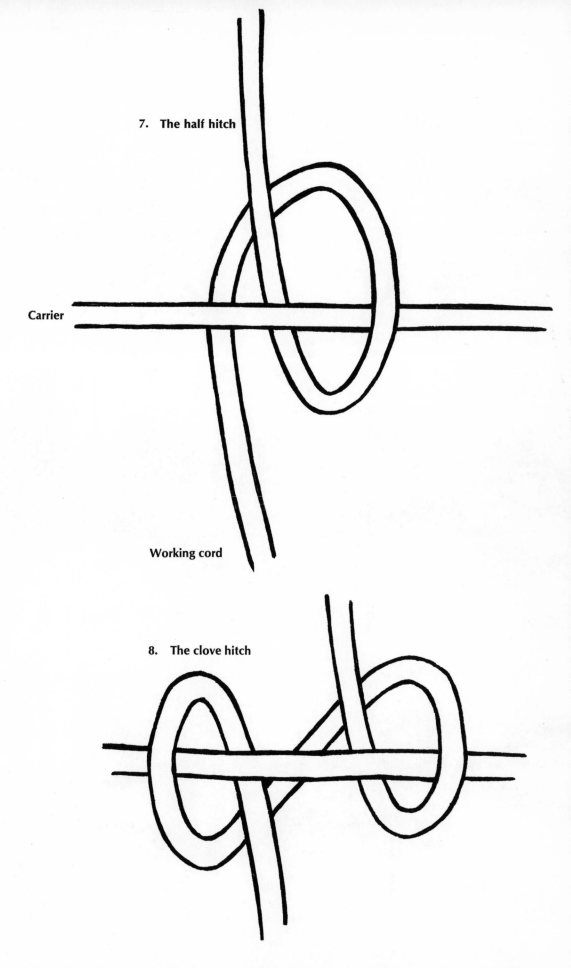

7.   The half hitch

Carrier

Working cord

8.   The clove hitch

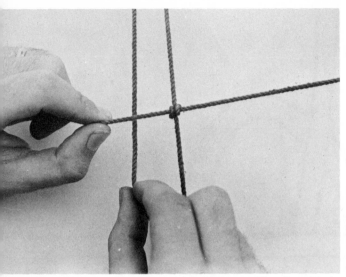
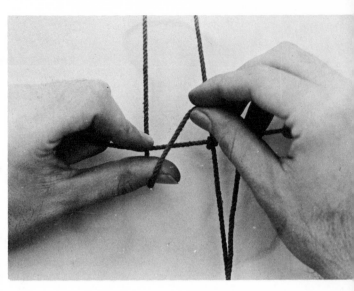

Figure 1   The clove hitch.

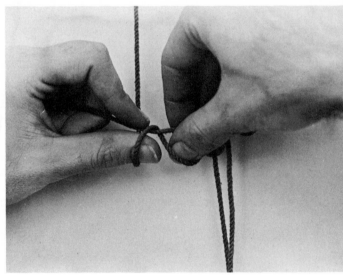

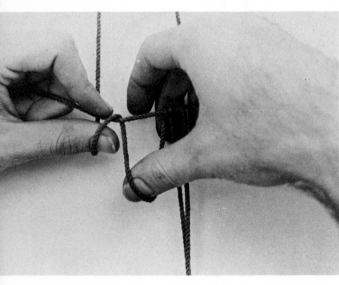
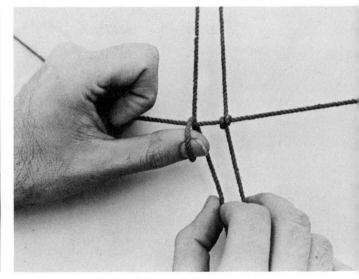

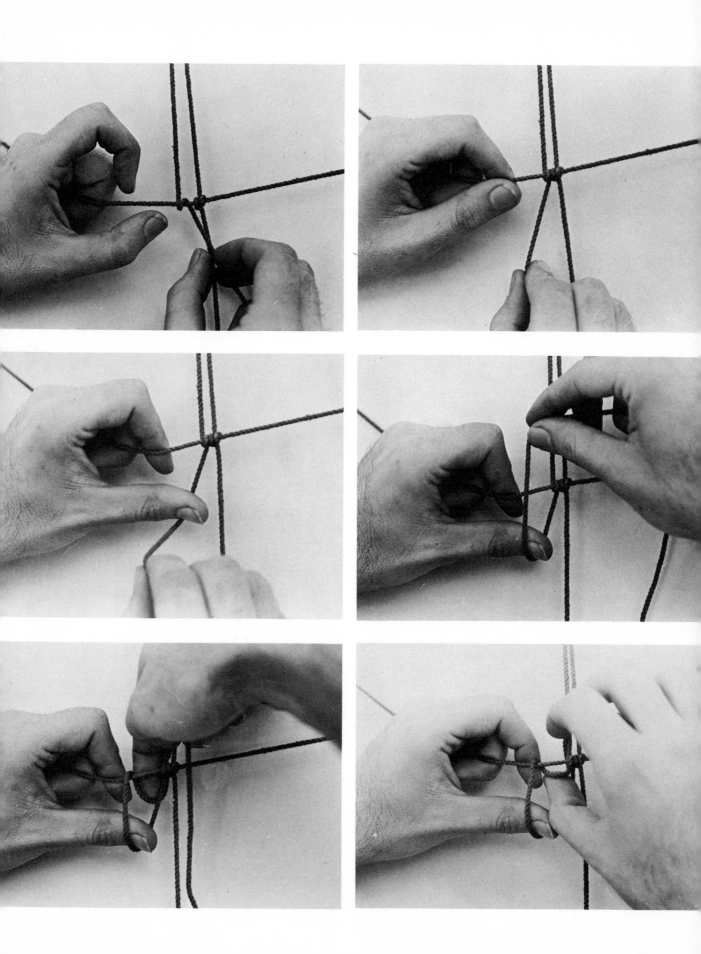

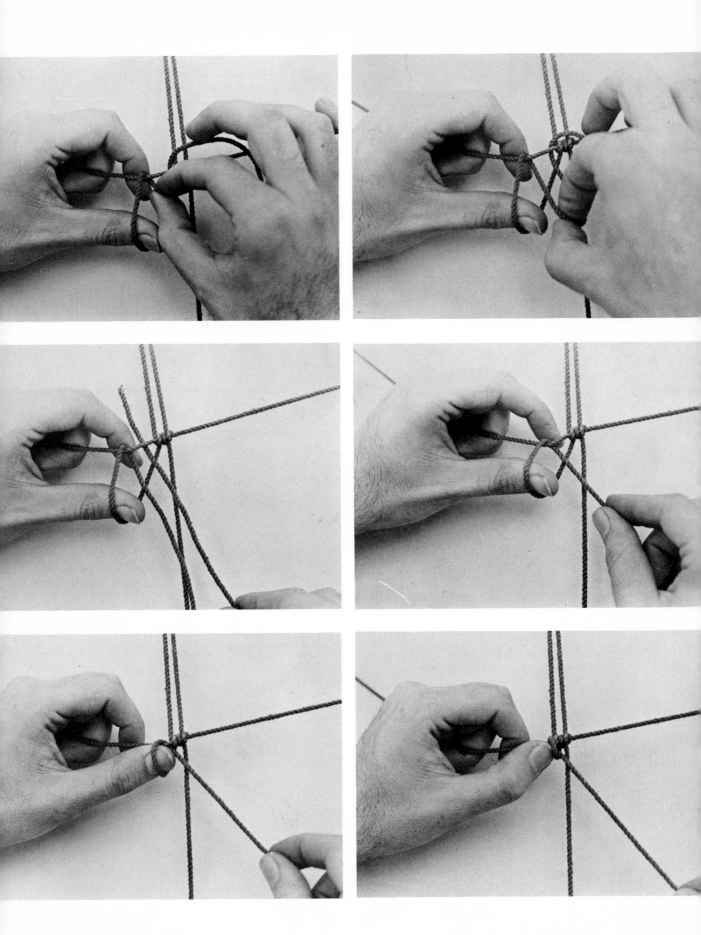

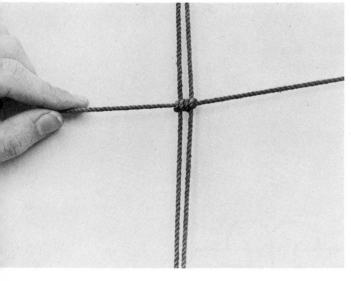

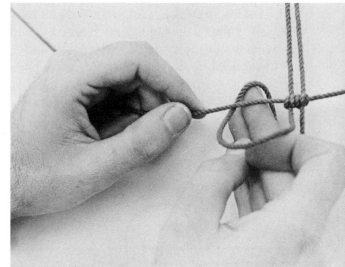

Figure 2   The clove hitch is followed by a half hitch.

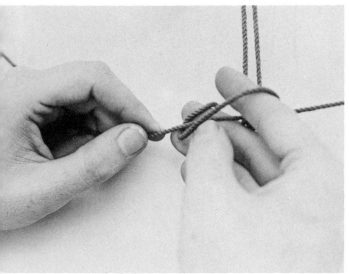

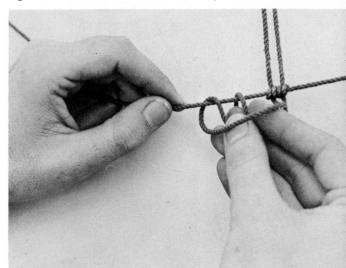

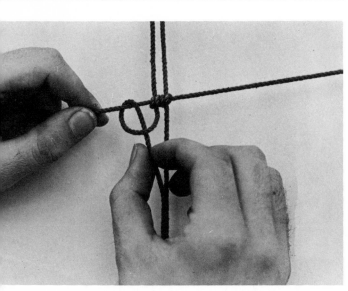

The second principal variation of the half hitch is the *lark's head* (also called a double half hitch) in which the direction of the working cord reverses (see Diagram 9 and Figure 3). You will begin most of the projects in this book by hitching working cords to carriers or bars with lark's head knots, and the same knot will be used along the side edges of several pieces.

9.   The lark's head

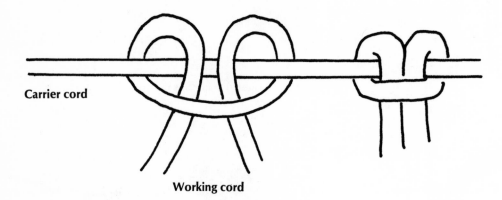

Carrier cord

Working cord

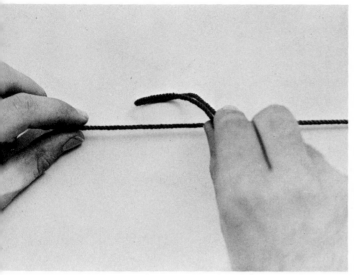

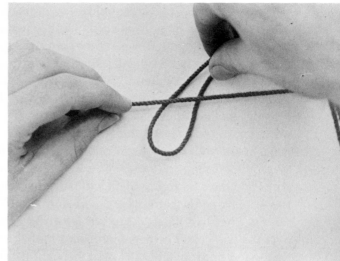

Figure 3   Hitching on cord for the lark's head knot.

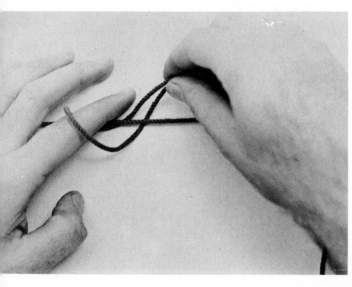

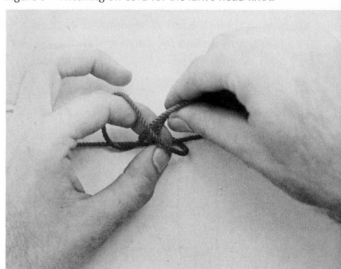

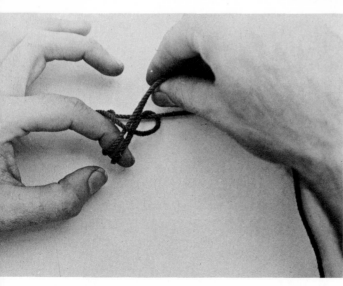

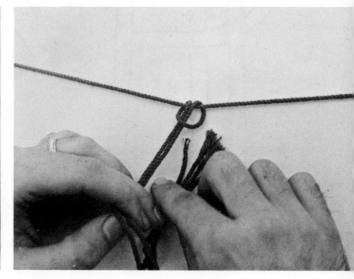

The macramé *square knot,* unlike the ordinary square knot, is tied over supporting carrier cords. Usually two *working cords* tie a square knot around two *carrier cords,* but more cords are sometimes used in ornamental knotting. Two ways to tie the square knot are illustrated in Figures 4 and 5. I prefer the first method shown because it is better for use with heavy cord.

In this method, the knot is tied in two steps, each consisting of two parts. To practice the knot, rig a horizontal cord on a tying board and attach two doubled cords with lark's heads to produce four tying cords. The center two will be carrier cords and must be kept straight and taut; the outer two will be the working cords that tie the square knot around the carriers. Tie the knot like this: (1) Lay the left-hand cord (number 1) over the two center carriers (numbers 2 and 3) and behind the right-hand cord (number 4); pass the right-hand cord behind the carrier cords and out the elbow of the left-hand cord. (2) Lay the right-hand cord (number 1) over the carrier cords and behind the left-hand cord (number 4); pass the left-hand cord (number 4) behind the carriers and out the elbow on the right. After positioning knot on the carrier cords, tighten it.

10.

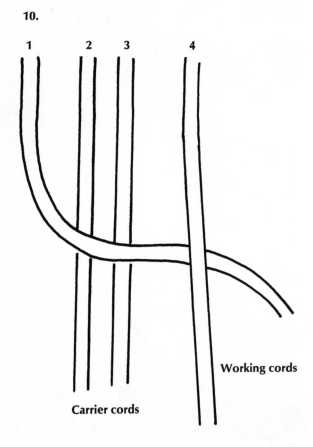

1   2   3   4

Working cords

Carrier cords

11.

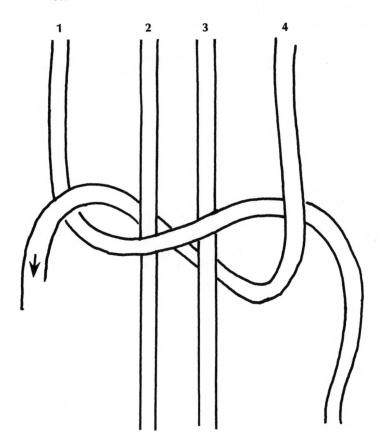

12.

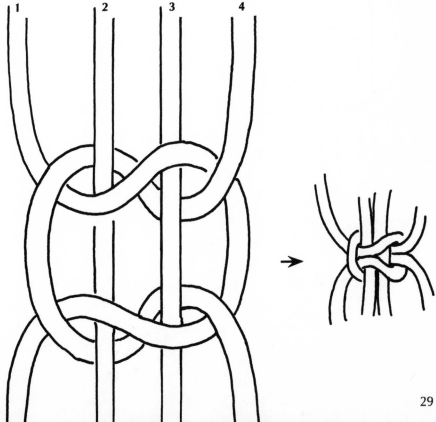

A square knot is always tied in two parts. Later we will vary the order of tying to produce versions other than the one shown here.

As you will see, most of our projects are finished in fringe. If you don't like fringe, the remainder cords may be clipped close to the last row of knots or sewn to seam binding and turned up in a hem.

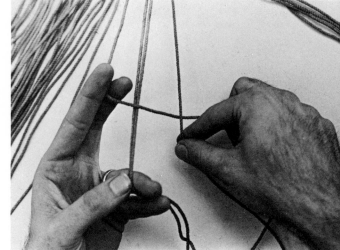

Figure 4   The macramé square knot.

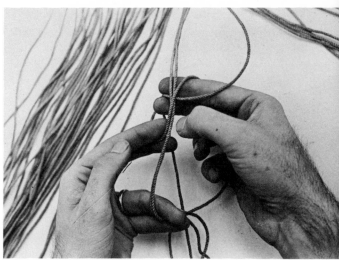

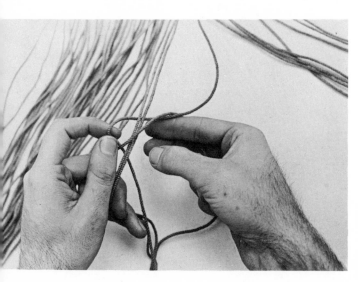

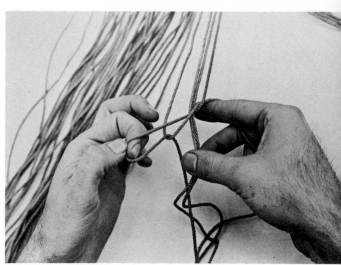

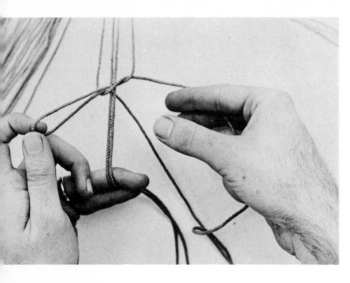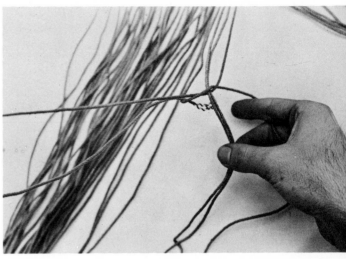

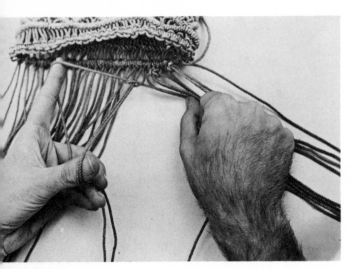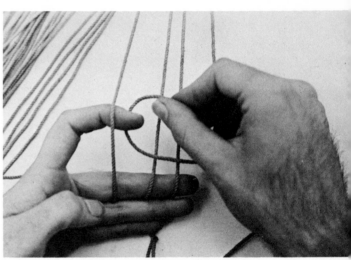

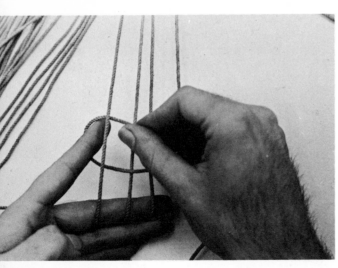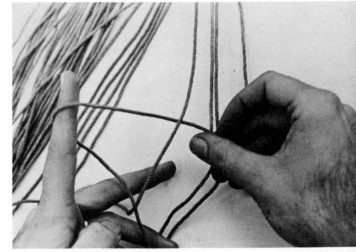

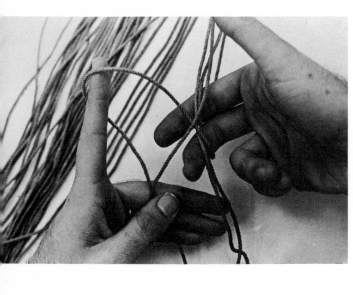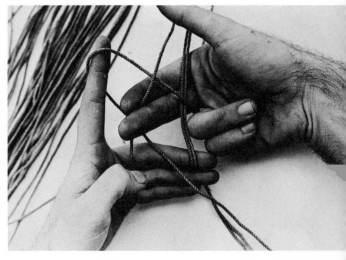
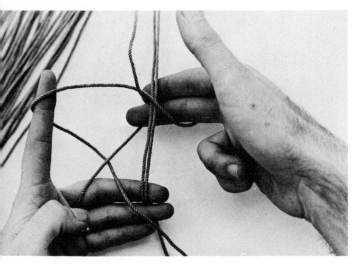
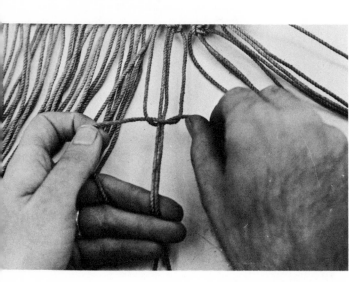

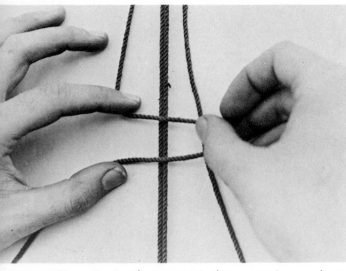

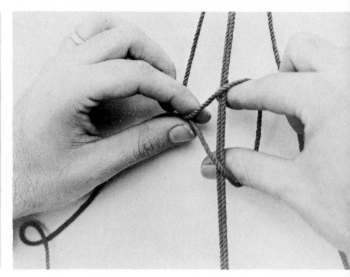

Figure 5   Another way to tie the macramé square knot.

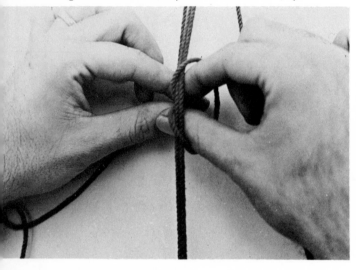

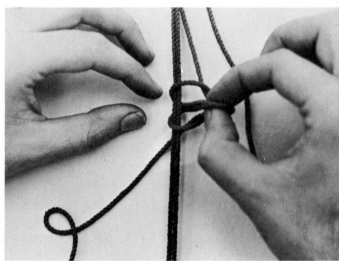

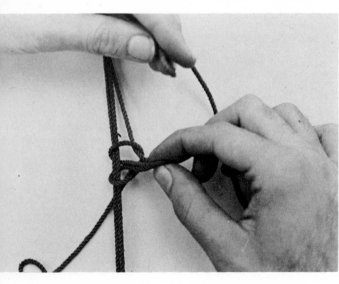

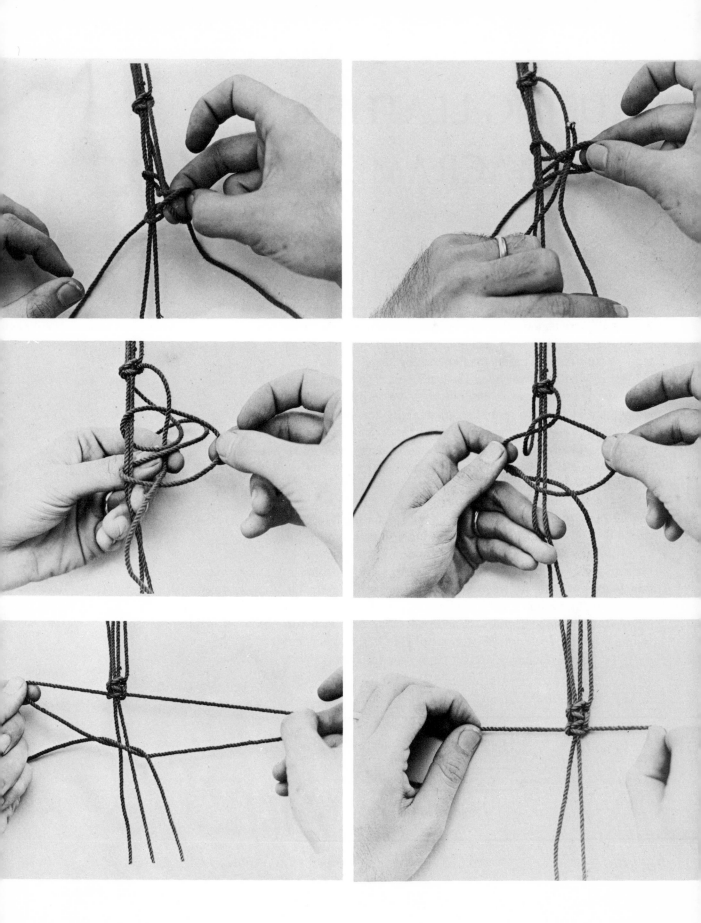

3 USING LEATHER IN MACRAMÉ

Leather enhances the appearance of many macramé pieces, especially belts and sashes. Since several of the projects we will do may use leather, this chapter contains some instructions on how to make your own leather closures. Fortunately, leather work is considerably easier than knot-tying.

Most of what you will need for leather work is inexpensive and easy to find. For example, old belts will provide enough leather and buckles for several macramé belts. Scraps of leather can also be obtained from shoe repair shops and stores that specialize in making leather goods. You will need some rivets (leather workers use two-part rivets, but regular aluminum or copper ones will do), a single-edged razor blade to cut the leather, and a hole punch. If you wish, you can invest in a leather punch for about three dollars, but a nail file, ice pick, or the drill on a Swiss army knife will serve the same purpose.

To prepare leather for a macramé belt, cut a strip about 12 inches long and the right width to pass through the buckle. Punch and cut a slot for the prong of the buckle (Diagram 13). Fold the leather around the fastening bar, punch two holes for the rivets to hold the buckle fast, and rivet (Diagram 14). If you want a leather loop to hold the tongue of your belt in place, cut

13.

Cut out with razor blade

Punch to round ↑

14. Two-part leather rivet

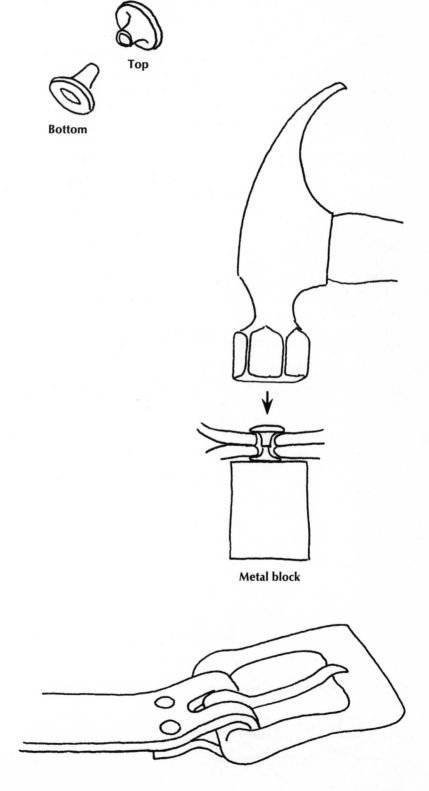

Top

Bottom

Metal block

an additional piece of leather ½ inch wide and long enough to encircle the belt. Punch two rivet holes in belt where loop will go, and two more in loop. Match the holes and rivet. Do not hesitate to hammer on the leather of the loop to secure the second rivet (Diagram 15).

In Diagram 16, a leather tongue is prepared for finishing a macramé belt. Working cords from the belt will be threaded through the holes in the tongue and knotted on the wrong side. In Diagram 17 are two macramé sashes finished with leather at both ends. Here again, cords are threaded through holes and knotted, and additional cord is cut for laces. The working cords may also be continued through as ties. Both of these sash styles can be tied either in front or back.

15.

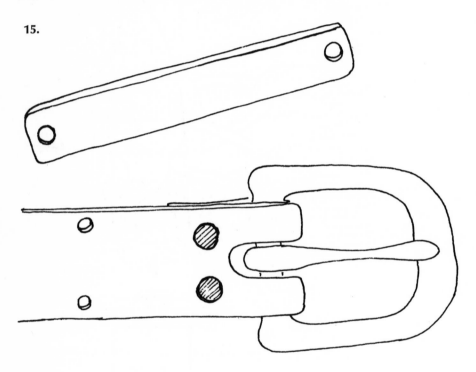

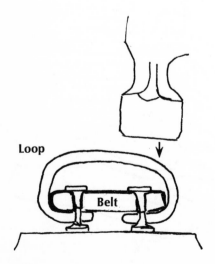

Loop

Belt

16.

17.

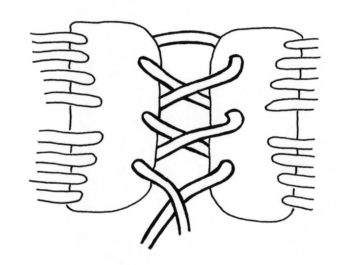

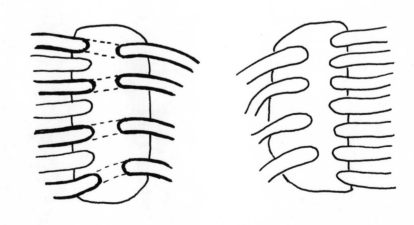

4 TWO SIMPLE BELTS

These two belts are tied using only the macramé square knot. Belt A is of repeated square knots; belt B varies the pattern slightly. Both belts are finished with leather buckles and tongues.

Instructions for Belt A   You will need two 15-foot lengths of No. 72 cotton seine twine, buckle with leather and leather tongue, and white glue.

Prepare the leather ends, punching four holes in each. Thread two cords through the buckle end to make four working cords and adjust them so the two center cords are about 3 feet long and the outer ones are 12 feet long. The center cords are carriers and outers are working cords. Tie the macramé square knot repeatedly until the belt is the desired length. Finish by threading cords through holes in tongue, knot, and trim cords close. To be sure knots will hold, coat them with glue.

Figure 6   Two simple macramé belts. Belt A on the left is made up of continuous square knots; belt B on the right is also square-knotted, but cords are alternated between knots.

Correctly tied, your belt should lie flat, the way it does in Diagram 18. If you forget to complete both steps in the square knot, however, and tie only the first part repeatedly, the result will be the twisted pattern illustrated in Diagram 19. This is often used in decorative macramé, but it does not make a good belt.

Instructions for Belt B You will need two 24-foot lengths of No. 72 cord, buckle with leather and tongue, and white glue.

Prepare buckle and leather as for belt A. Thread the cord through the buckle leather, but make the cords of equal length. In this pattern, the carrier and working cords will be reversed after each knot. Complete your first square knot and swing the outer working cords into the center to make them carriers. Tie the second square knot around them with the other two cords. Reverse cords after each knot and continue until belt is the desired length. Finish like belt A.

This pattern eliminates a chronic difficulty in macramé: the unequal consumption of cord that occurs in repeating the square knot. The macramé belt in the next chapter also uses square knots in a way that avoids this problem.

18.   The square knot

19.   Square knot twist

20.   Reversing the carrier and working cords

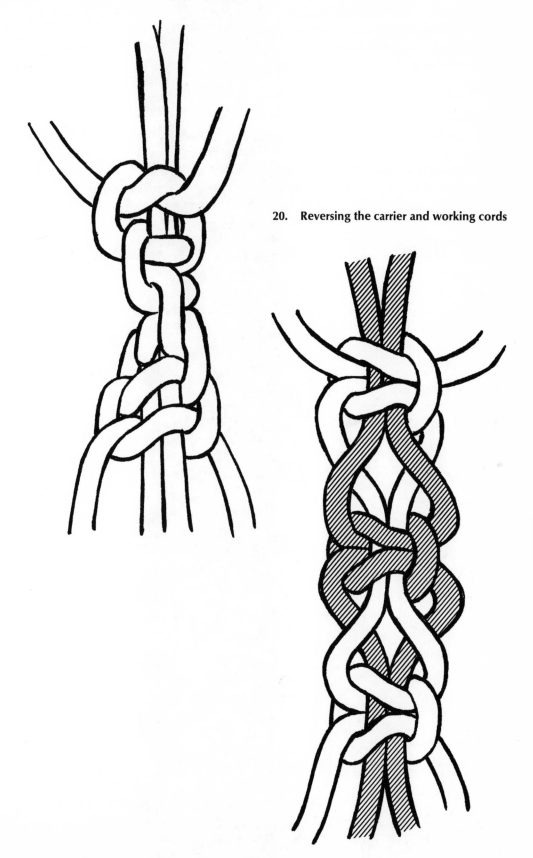

5 A MACRAMÉ BELT

Another variation of the square knot is produced by inverting the two steps used in tying it. I call this "new" knot a right-hand square knot, and the ordinary macramé square knot a left-hand knot. Both knots will be used in this belt. In future instructions when I say square knot, tie the left-handed knot. Only the right-hand knot will be specified.

The instructions are for a belt without leather, but the pattern is also good for sash belts. It is particularly striking when cords of more than one color are used.

Instructions   You will need four 32-foot lengths of No. 72 cotton seine twine and a belt buckle about 1 to 1¼ inches wide.

Hitch four doubled cords over the carrier bar of the buckle, two on each side of the buckle prong. Tie the left-hand four cords in a square knot. The right-hand four cords will now be tied in reverse to make the *right-hand square knot*. To tie the right-hand knot, pass the right-hand cord over the carrier cords and behind the left-hand cord, bringing the left-hand cord behind the carrier cords and out the elbow of the right-hand cord. Then carry the left-hand cord over the carrier cords and behind the right-hand cord, bringing the right-hand cord behind the carrier cords and out the elbow of the left-hand cord (see Diagram 21).

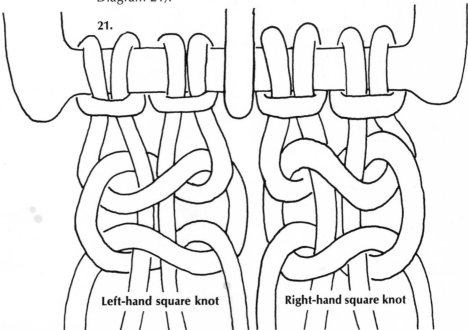

Left-hand square knot   **Right-hand square knot**

Figure 7   A macramé belt using left- and right-hand knot.

Tie a left-hand square knot with four center cords, as shown in Diagram 22, and finish the edges with two lark's head knots. Hitch the inner cords of each pair over outer ones as shown in Diagram 23. This completes the basic pattern.

Repeat these two rows until you have a belt of the desired length (32-foot cords will give you enough for a 38-inch belt).

22.

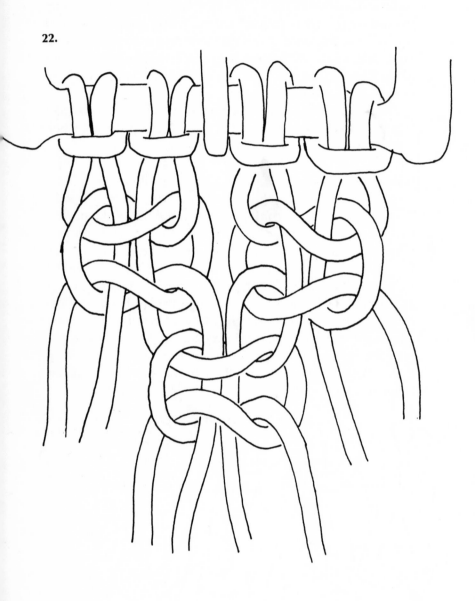

23.

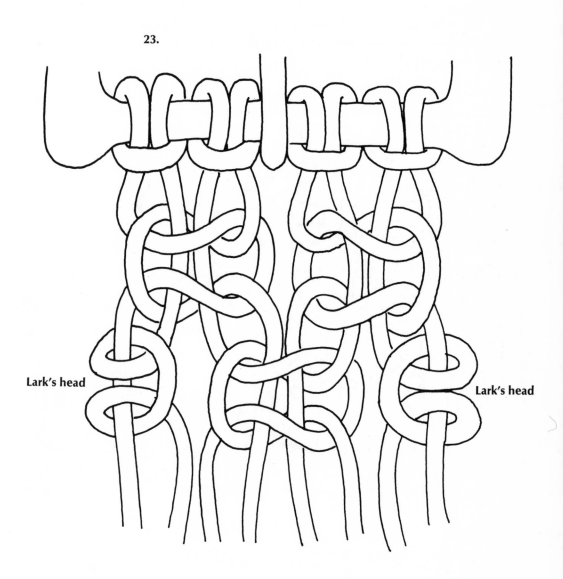

Lark's head   Lark's head

To finish the belt, end the pattern on the second row and tie an overhand knot in the outermost cords, close to the lark's heads. Trim these two cords (Diagram 24). Tie overhand knots in the two working cords of the central square knot of the last row and trim these cords (Diagram 25). Tie a second square knot over the center carrier cords, using the two edge cords as working cords. Tie overhand knots in all four cords and trim (Diagram 26).

The belt threads directly through the buckle, and the buckle prong pierces the pattern between the center square knots. If you make this belt with leather ends, you can fit the required eight holes on a narrow tab by punching them in a diagonal rather than a straight line.

24.

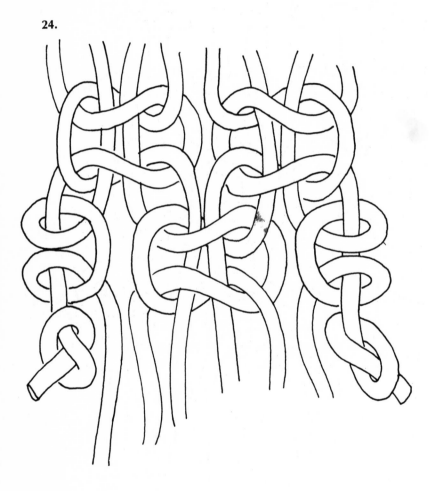

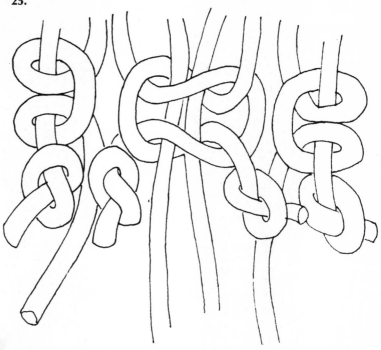

6 FANCY MACRAMÉ BELTS

The two belts in this chapter have openwork patterns that alternate the square knot with weaving. In both styles, nylon may be used for a dressier belt. I have called for more cord than you will need for each belt so you can vary the pattern if you wish, without fear of running out.

Instructions for Belt A   You will need four 14-foot lengths of No. 72 cord, a standard belt buckle mounted with leather, leather tongue, and leather loop.

Thread the cords through the leather to set up eight working cords. Tie a square knot and a right-hand square knot, as before (see Diagram 27), and then weave the four central cords

27.

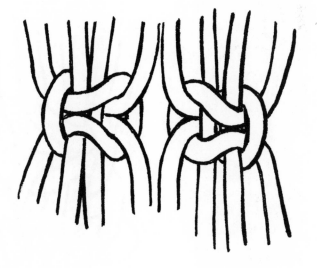

Figure 8   Fancy macramé belts. Two belts on the right are the same style done in nylon and in cotton cord. Nylon belt on the left is another version of square knot and weaving.

through each other (Diagram 28). Tie a lark's head knot with the two cords on either side (Diagram 29) and repeat pattern for desired length (Diagram 30).

Finish by threading end cords through holes in leather tongue. If you're using nylon, you must knot and melt the ends to prevent slipping.

28.

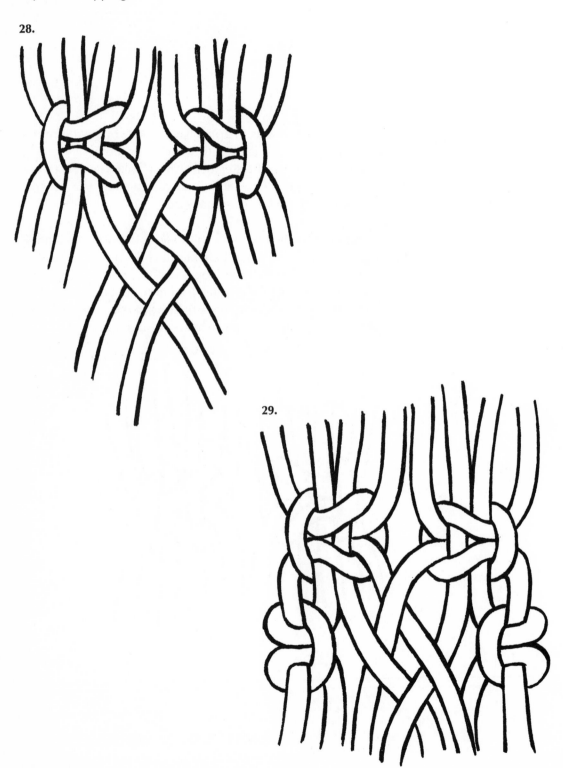

29.

30.

Instructions for Belt B   Set up eight working cords. Tie a square knot with the four center cords, about ½ inch from the leather edge (Diagram 31). Tie a right-hand square knot with the left four cords and a square knot with the right four cords (Diagram 32). Tie two lark's head knots on edges, as usual (Diagram 33), and weave the center four cords. Tie a right-hand square knot with the four cords on the left and a square knot with the cords on the right (Diagram 34). Close the circle with a right-hand

31.

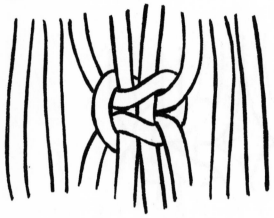

32.

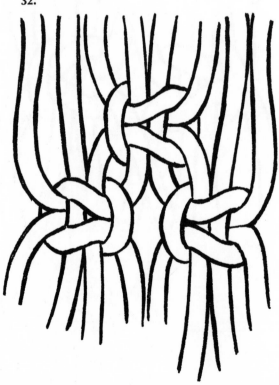

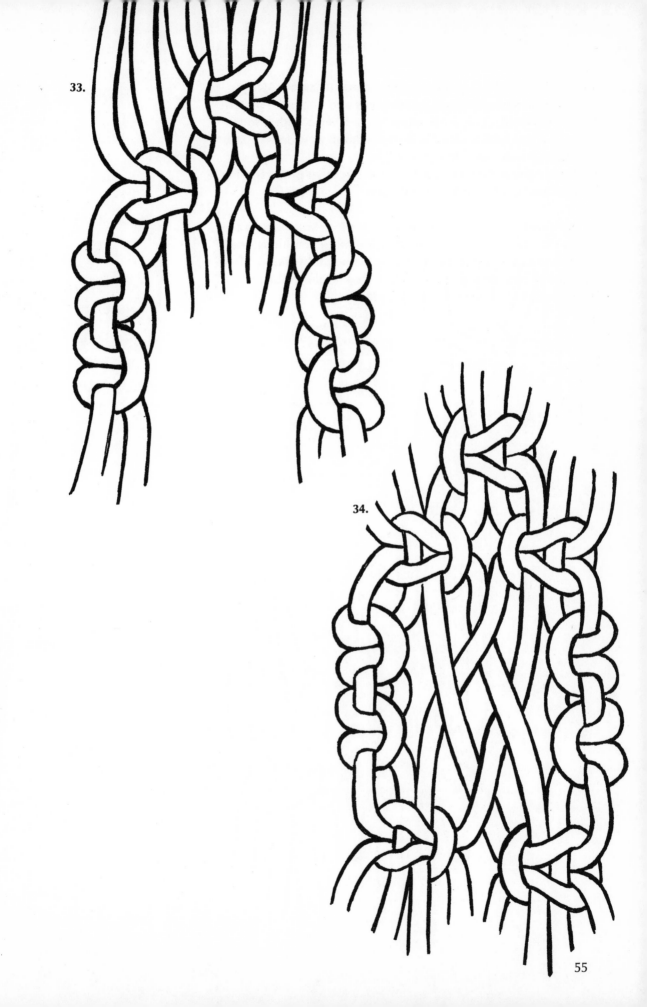

33.

34.

square knot tied with the center four cords (Diagram 35).

Reverse the working and carrier cords and begin the pattern again. Correctly done, each ellipse should begin with a square knot and end with a right-hand square knot, as it does in Diagram 36. Finish like belt A.

This elliptical design is suitable for use in other projects using almost any number of additional cords.

Now that you have completed this project, you possess the basic macramé skills necessary to tackle more ambitious ones. Make use of the techniques you have learned to work up a few designs of your own and then take a look at the color section of this book for some other design ideas.

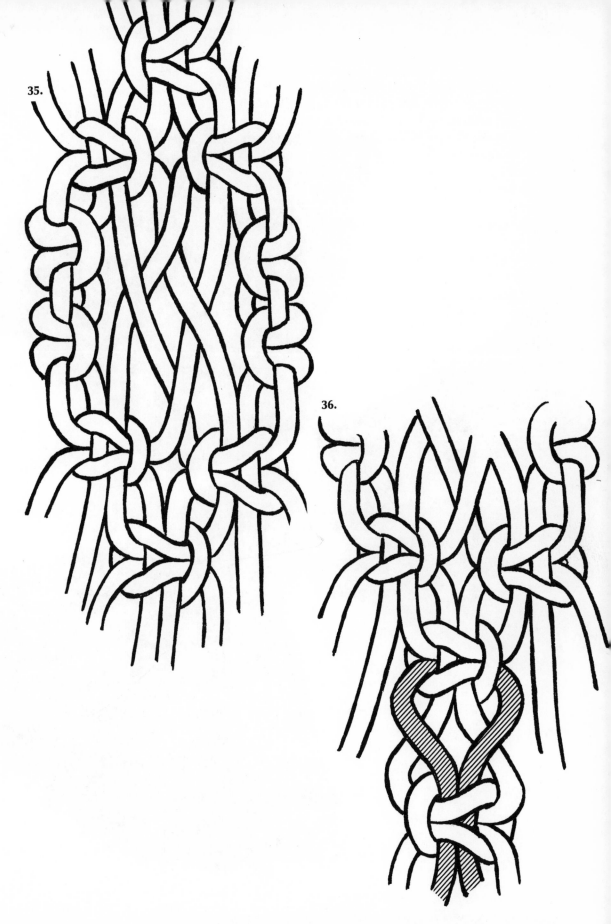

35.

36.

Working and carrier cords are reversed, and pattern is repeated

Figure 9   Three variations of the macramé hat. By loosening tension
between knots you can fashion a hat with a fuller brim.

7 A MACRAMÉ HAT

In this piece the square knot is used in a pattern of concentric circles. The number of working cords is increased as you work, to shape the hat. This pattern is a bit more difficult than any of the ones you have done before, but the techniques, once mastered, will be useful.

Instructions You will need eighty 10-foot lengths of cotton seine twine (choose any thickness from No. 36 to 42). A tying board will not be used.

Start with five cords. Lay the first cord over your knee in a circle, as is done in Diagram 37. Double the other four cords,

37.

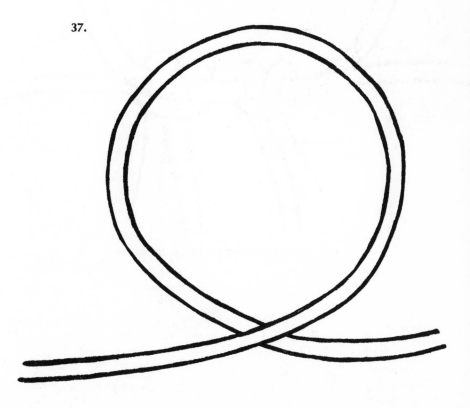

hitch them over the circular carrier, as in Diagram 38, and pull the ends of the carrier cord to tighten (Diagram 39). The leading end of the carrier cord will continue to be used as carrier cord for the second row of knots; the other end will be used later as a working cord. Begin the second row by hitching a doubled cord over the carrier cord (Diagram 40). Clove-hitch

38.

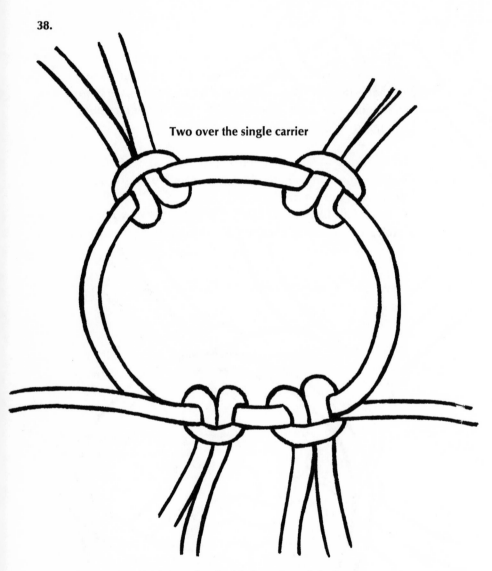

Two over the single carrier

Two over the doubled portion of the carrier

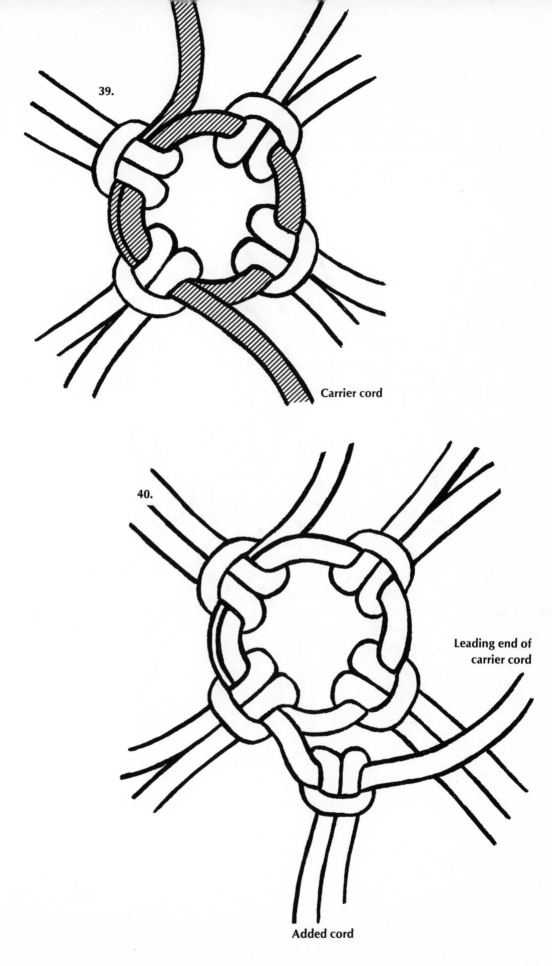

39.

Carrier cord

40.

Leading end of
carrier cord

Added cord

the first two working cords of the first row over the carrier cord of the second row, using the clove hitch followed by a half hitch, as illustrated in Diagram 41. Add another doubled cord and then hitch the next two working cords from the first row over the carrier (Diagram 42). Continue around the circle in this manner, adding a new doubled cord before each pair of working cords. When you reach the other end of your first-row

41.

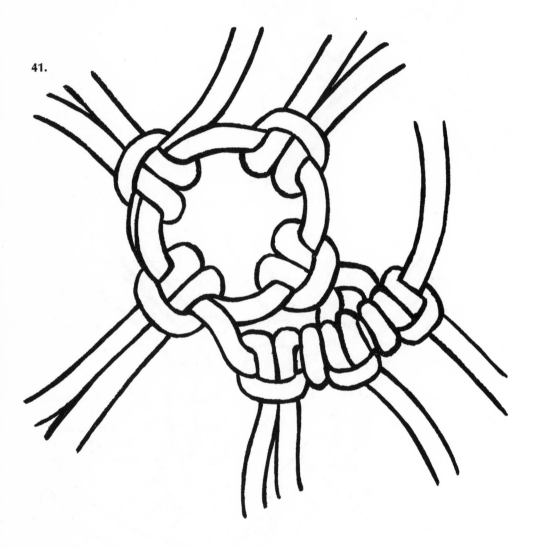

42.

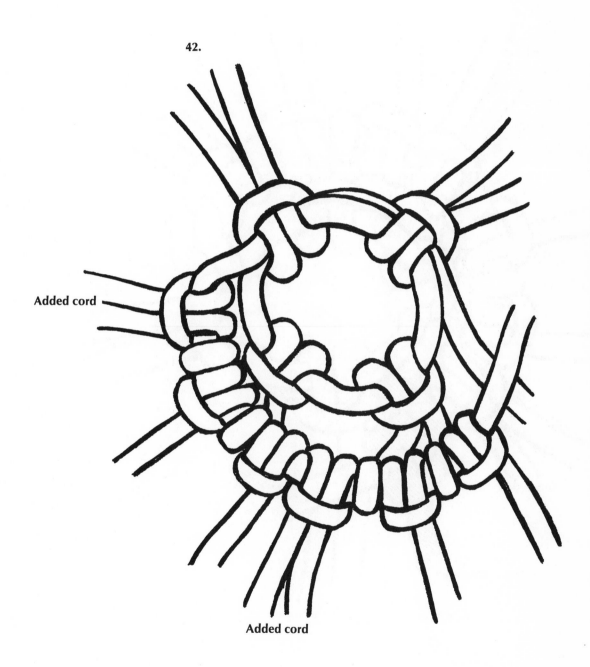

Added cord

Added cord

carrier, tie it over the second-row carrier with a clove and half hitch (Diagrams 43 and 44), counting it as the first of that pair of working cords. Note that when you add your next doubled cord, you will be splitting up a pair of working cords from the

43.

Added cord

Added cord

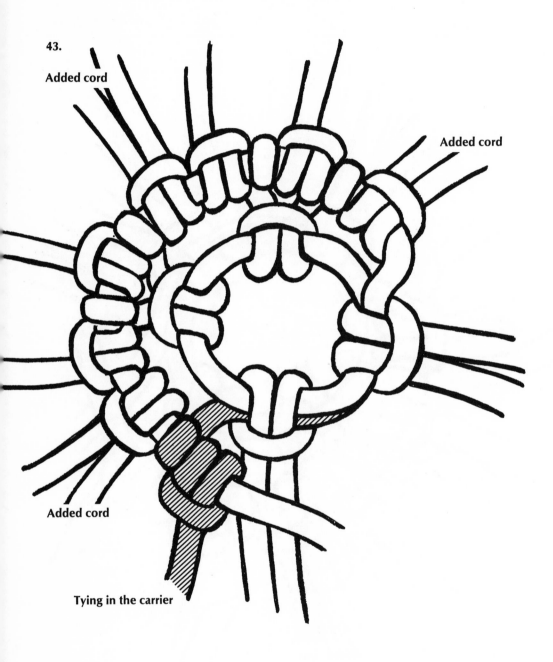

Added cord

Tying in the carrier

44.

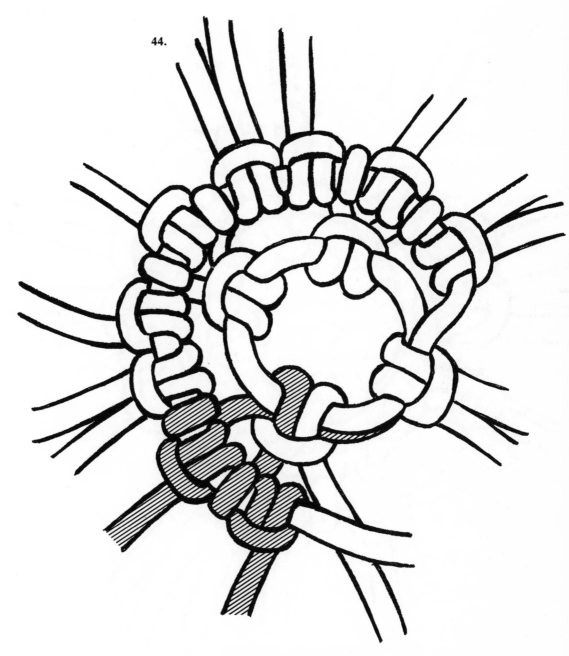

Now you are splitting up original pair of working cords

first row. Work around the circle, keeping the knots tight and the second row drawn in close to the first. After you have added the fifth doubled cord to the row, there will be one working cord left from the first row. Hitch this over the carrier cord, and count it and the carrier as the last pair of working cords. There are now twenty working cords (Diagram 45).

45.

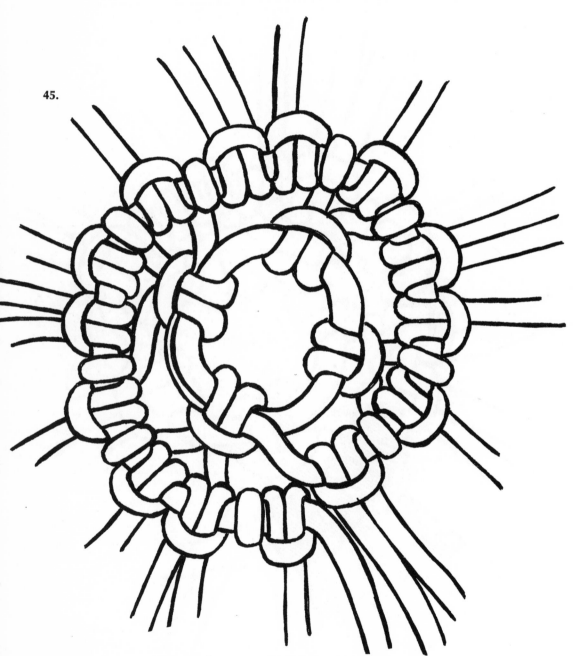

You now have 20 cords, counting the carrier

The next part is tied in the alternating square knot pattern which is used in many macramé pieces. Begin with a square knot tied across the juncture of the second row, using two cords from each side of the juncture. This knot stabilizes the second row. Tie four more square knots around the circle, as illustrated in Diagram 46.

46.

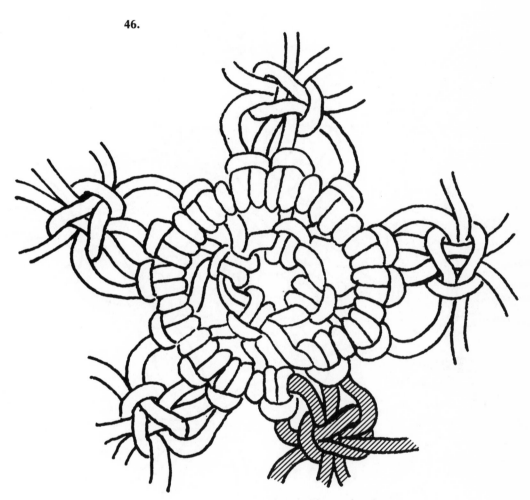

Start with a square knot

Tie a second row of square knots, alternating with the preceding row. Take two cords from each of two adjacent knots in the row above for the four cords you need to tie each square knot (Diagram 47).

47.

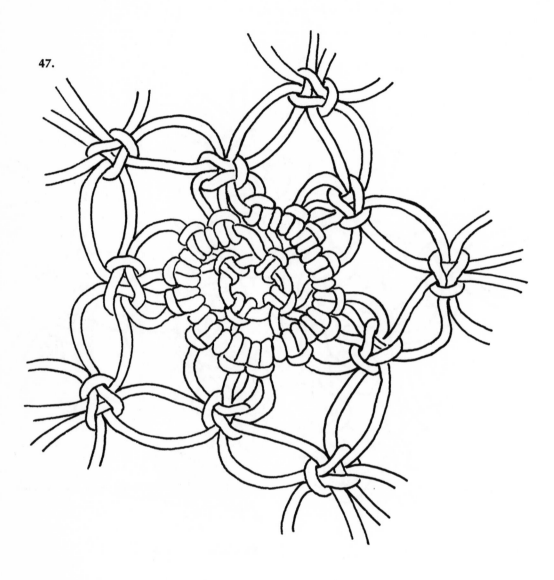

Add twenty working cords to the pattern by threading two cords through each pair of loops between the rows of square knots (see Diagram 48). Use each set of added cords to tie a

48.

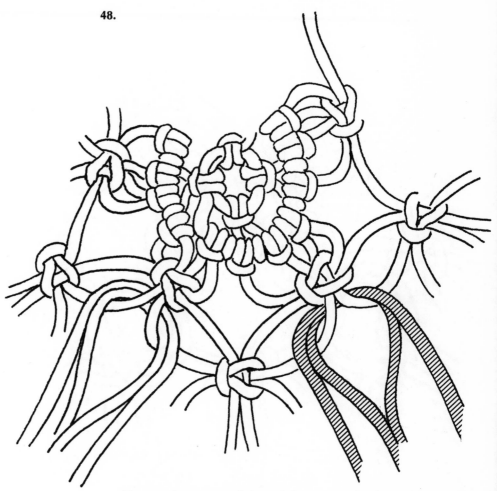

Two cords are passed through loops to make four added cords

square knot, as in Diagram 49. Tie two more rows of the alternating square knot pattern with the 40 working cords. As you tie, adjust the tension and spacing of the knots to make a gently curving dome shape. Add another 40 working cords (to make 80 working cords) in the same manner as before.

49.

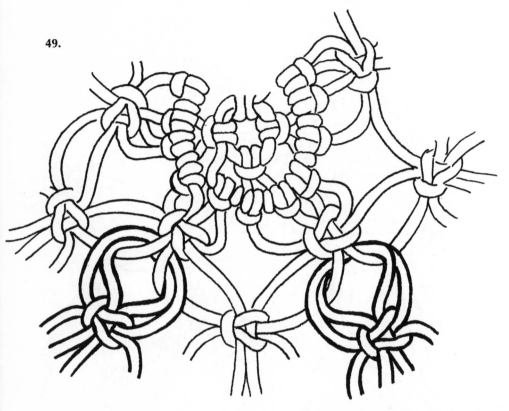

The square knots with added cords

The crown of the hat is tied in a basket-weave pattern. Eight rows of basket weave (equivalent to sixteen rows of alternating square knots) are required. Each row of basket-weave pattern has two parts. First, two cords from each adjacent pair of square knots in the last row are interwoven (as in the belts in Chapter 6). Then, a row of square knots is tied, as in Diagram 50. Each square knot lies directly below a knot in the preceding knotted row (rather than between, as in the alternating square knot pattern), and each is tied of cords originating in the knots to either side of the knot it underlies. While tying the eight rows of basket-weave pattern, gradually loosen the pattern so that the crown of the hat will taper slightly (see Figure 9).

50.

One basket-weave pattern equals two square knot rows

Figure 10   A wide-brimmed macramé hat.

After the last row of basket weave, tie one row of square knots, alternating with the knots of the last basket-weave row.

Again double the number of working cords (to 160) by adding 40 doubled cords (80 working cords) through the loops between the last two rows of square knots.

Tie four rows of basket-weave pattern. Because of the last increase, the hat should flare out to form the brim.

Next, tie a single row of double basket-weave pattern (Diagram 51). This pattern is similar to the ordinary basket weave, except that there are two weaving steps between rows of square knots.

Three rows of basket weave, one of double basket weave, and two rows of alternating square knots finish the brim. Tie overhand knots close to the last row of square knots and trim the cords.

51.

Double basket weave equals three rows of square knots

Figure 11   The macramé shoulder purse.

8 A MACRAMÉ SHOULDER PURSE

Instructions   You will need seventy-seven 7-foot lengths and four 24-foot lengths of No. 36 cotton seine twine. A tying board will be used.

Rig a single horizontal carrier cord across the middle of the board. The purse layout is illustrated in Diagram 52.

52.

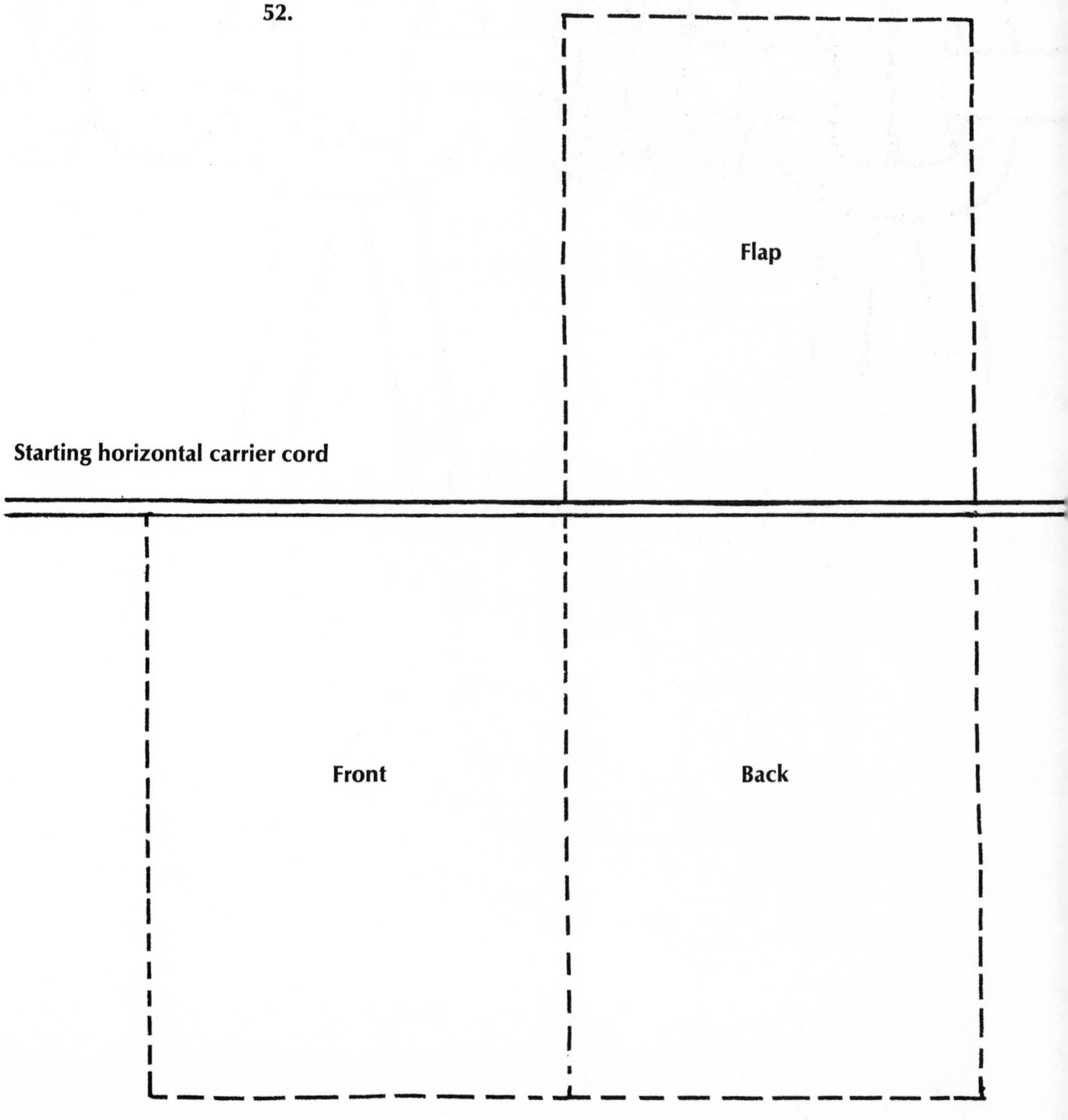

Flap

Starting horizontal carrier cord

Front

Back

For the front, hitch 24 doubled cords over the carrier cord. Using another cord as spacer, hitch lark's head knots from above between each of the 24 cords (Diagram 53). Tie overhand knots in the ends of the spacer cord and trim.

53.

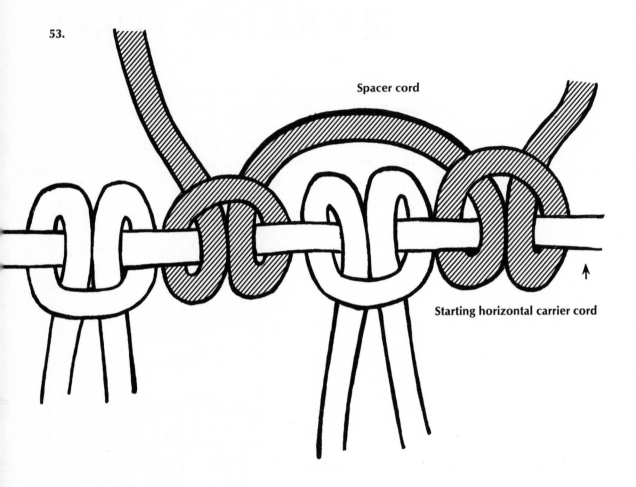

Spacer cord

Starting horizontal carrier cord

Set up the back by hitching on 24 doubled cords, alternating with 23 doubled cords hitched on from above to make the flap (Diagram 54). Fasten another horizontal carrier cord to the board about ½ inch below the first and clove-hitch all the cords of the front and back over it (Diagram 55).

54.

This will be the flap

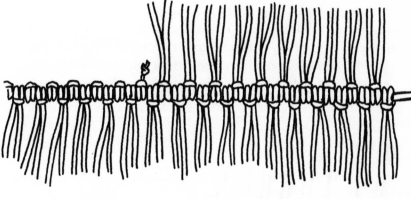

Front   **Purse back**

55.

Starting carrier cord

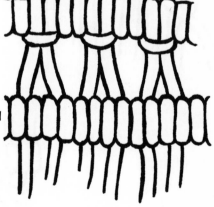

Second horizontal carrier cord

The diamond pattern along the upper border of the purse is tied as repeating X's in 12 groups of 8 cords. You may start tying the X's in the center or at either end, but each is tied in the same way. In each group of 8 cords, the edge cords are used as carrier cords, and the central 6 cords are clove-hitched over them. To tie the pattern, hold the right-hand cord diagonally over the other 7 cords (Diagram 56) and clove-hitch the next 3 cords over it. Hold the left-hand cord in similar manner and clove-hitch the remaining 3 cords over it (Diagram 57). Cross the carrier cords by clove-hitching the left cord over the right and continue each down to complete the X, hitching the working cords over the appropriate carrier (Diagram 58).

Tie 12 such X's across the purse. Add a third horizontal carrier cord just below the X's and clove-hitch all the working cords over it (Diagram 59).

56.

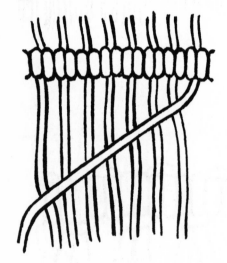

57.

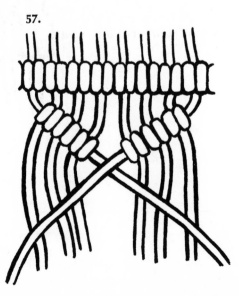

58.

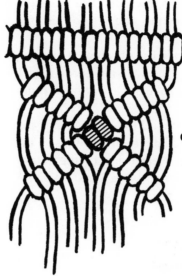

Clove-hitch left carrier cord over right
carrier cord at juncture

59.

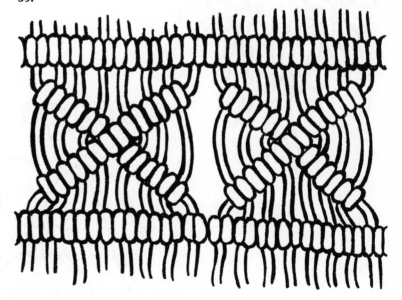

The body of the purse is tied in the alternating square knot pattern, leaving about ⅜ inch between rows. Because the edges will not be finished until later, taper the sides as you tie (see Diagram 60).

When the purse is the desired depth, usually about 12 inches, finish the pattern by clove-hitching the working cords over a fourth horizontal carrier cord (Diagram 61). Do *not* hitch outer cords that haven't been tied.

Remove the purse from the tying board to join the front and back. Loosen the three or four clove hitches at the ends of the upper three carrier cords and thread each end of the carrier through the clove hitches on its other end (see Diagram 62). A

60. A

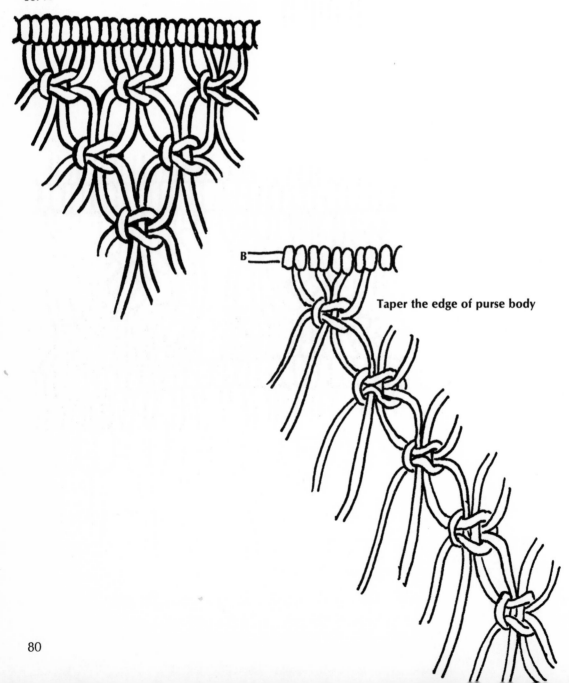

Taper the edge of purse body

61.

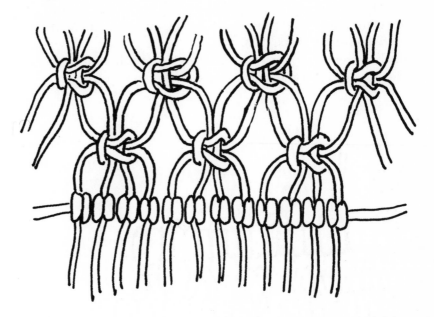

62. Passing the ends of the carrier cords through the loosened clove hitches

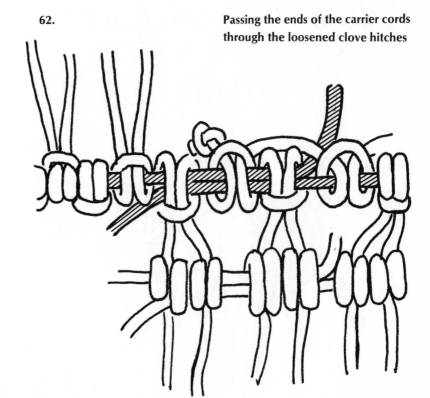

hemostat is very helpful in this maneuver. Tie overhand knots in the carrier cord ends and trim close. To fill in the area left by tapering the edges, continue the alternating square knot pattern around the seam (Diagram 63).

Hitch the remaining working cords over the fourth horizontal carrier cord and join ends as you did with the upper carriers.

63.

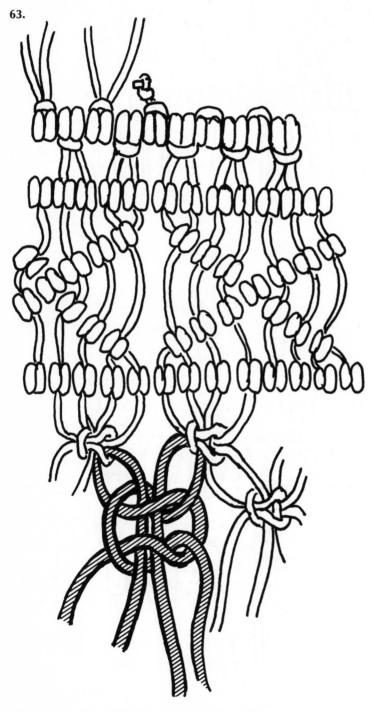

Filling in the tapered portions of the purse body

Close the bottom of the purse by clove-hitching a horizontal cord around groups of four working cords—two each from front and back (Diagram 64). Finish the cords as fringe by tying overhand knots and trimming to length.

64.   Closing the purse bottom.

The flap is tied in the alternating square knot pattern (Diagram 65 is a tying diagram of purse flap). The 46 working cords in the flap, however, cannot be evenly divided into groups of four to tie the first row of square knots. To avoid an asymmetric flap pattern, mark the center of the flap and tie a square knot on each side of it. Continuing out from the center, tie ten square knots in all, leaving three unused cords at each edge of the first row. Hitch the innermost of the three in a lark's head knot over the other two to complete the first row. When tying the second row of the pattern, leave the one cord remaining at each edge untied (see Diagram 66). Repeat the two rows twice more (total is six rows) and begin the diamond design.

65.   The purse flap

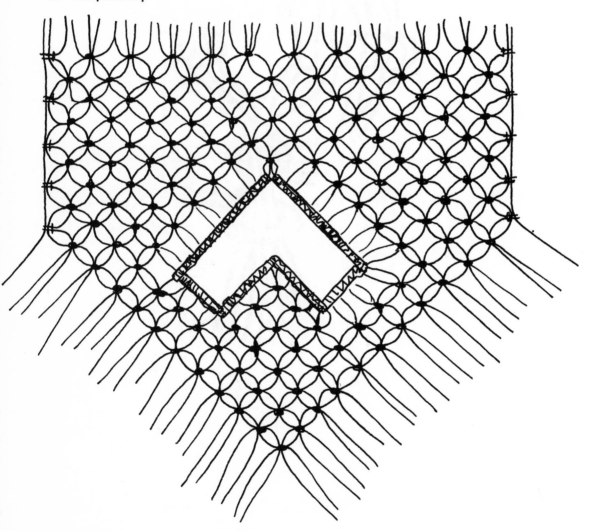

66.

As you tie the diamond pattern, you also continue the alternating square knot pattern down each side of it. After the sixth row of alternating square knots, the two center cords of the flap become the carrier cords of the upper edges of the diamond. The three cords on each side of them are clove-hitched over them as in Diagram 67. Continue tying the alternating square knot pattern down, taking two cords from each row of square knots to clove-hitch over the carrier cord of both sides, until eleven cords have been hitched over each carrier cord (Diagram 68).

Begin to taper the edge of the flap ten rows from the beginning (see Diagram 65). Taper by tying an overhand knot in the cord close to the last square knot and cutting to length as fringe.

67.

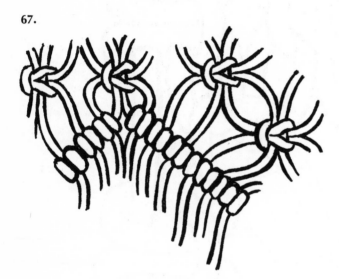

68.

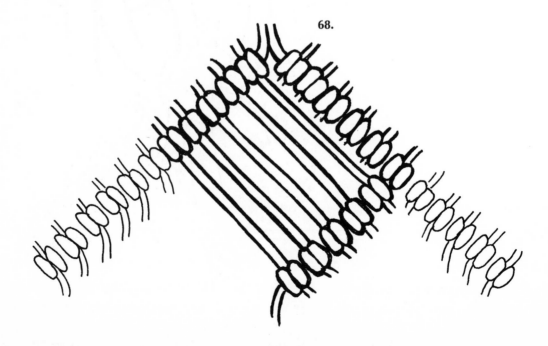

The sixth cord on each side is used as a carrier cord to close the upper diamond. Clove-hitch the five cords from the upper left side over the lower right carrier and then weave the five cords from the upper right side through them and clove-hitch over the lower left carrier. Hitch the left carrier over the right (Diagrams 68 and 69).

Tie two smaller diamonds below the first. Tie the left diamond by using the eleventh cord on the left side as a carrier cord and hitching over it the five cords of the lower left side of the first diamond (Diagram 70). Weave the four remaining

69.

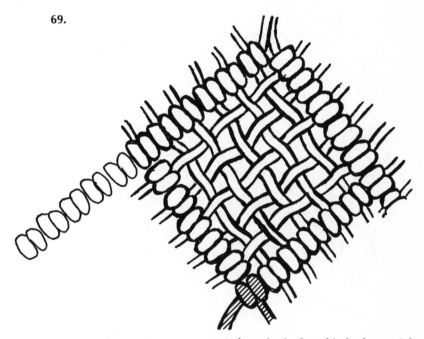

Left carrier is clove-hitched over right

70.

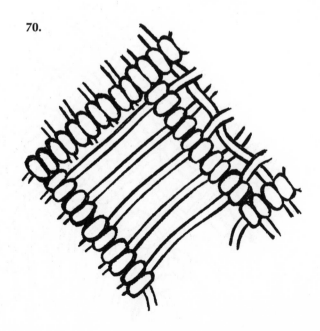

cords of the original eleven on that side through these five and
hitch them over the carrier cord of the lower right side of the
first diamond, which has been continued down to complete
the left diamond. Hitch the left carrier over the right (Diagram
71).

The right-hand diamond is tied in similar fashion (Diagram
72).

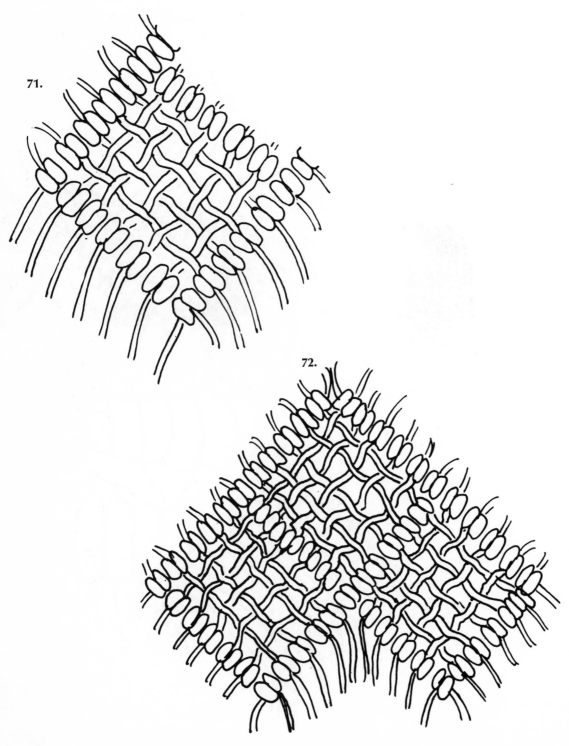

71.

72.

The alternating square knot pattern is used to fill in between the lower diamonds and continued down and around them to end the flap in a point, as indicated in the tying diagram.

Hitch the cords for the strap onto the upper carrier cord of the purse (Diagram 73). The strap may be tied in any pattern

73.   A 24-foot cord is used for the strap

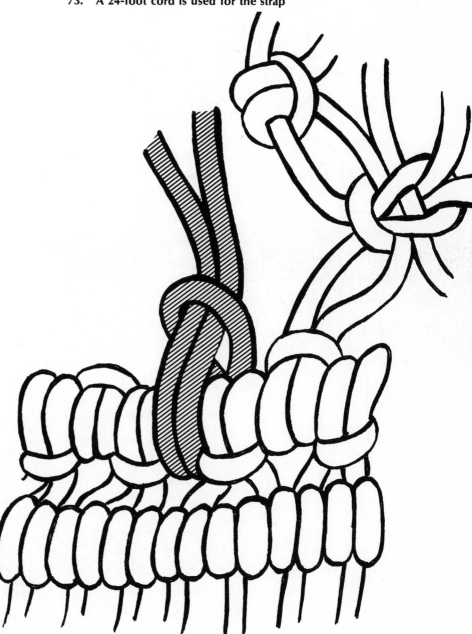

previously used for a belt, or in the alternating double lark's head pattern shown in Diagram 74.

After the strap is the desired length (usually 28 inches) it is joined to the other side of the purse as indicated in Diagram 75.

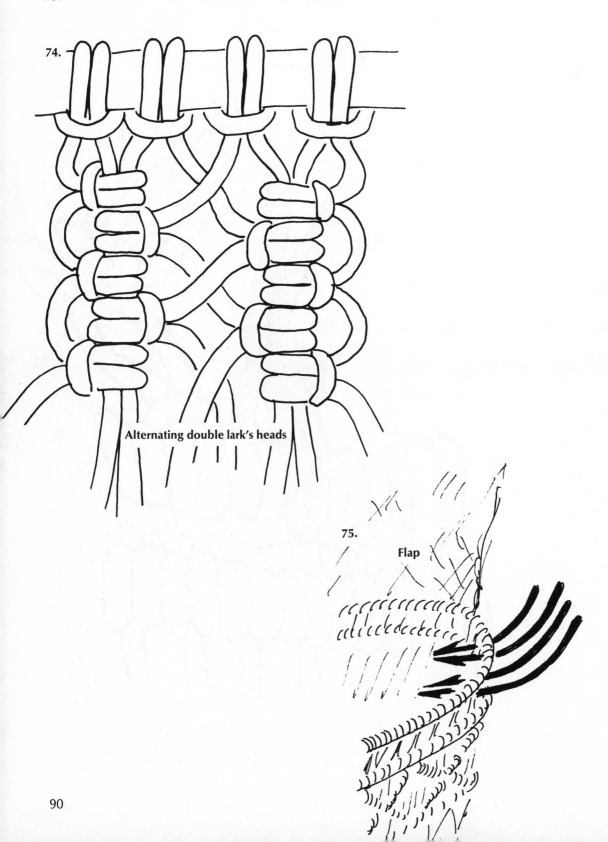

74.

Alternating double lark's heads

75.

Flap

Figure 12   Purse opened, showing pattern of front and flap.

Figure 13　The hairy purse with leather strap closings.

9 A HAIRY PURSE

Instructions You will need eighty 10-foot lengths of No. 42 cotton seine twine and two 20-foot lengths and one 4-foot length of No. 72 cotton seine twine.

Start with 5 cords, adding 5 more to complete the basic circle of 20 working cords explained in Chapter 7. Tie two rows of square knots, increasing 20 working cords to 40. Tie one row of square knots and add 40 more working cords. With the resulting 80 working cords, tie five rows of alternating square knot pattern and add 40 more cords for a final total of 160 working cords.

Tie two rows of alternating square knots to complete the bottom of the pouch, which should be about seven inches in diameter.

Tie two rows of basket-weave pattern, adjusting the tension so that the work will turn up to form the sides of the purse.

Separate the cords into four groups of 40 cords and mark the divisions between the groups with a bit of yarn or cord.

In the next part of the pattern, the purse will be tapered, and decreases in the number of working cords will be made along the four lines you have marked.

Nine rows of basket-weave pattern complete the tapered portion of the sides. Decreases are made in six of these rows, with each decrease removing four cords at each of the four borders you have marked.

Figure 14   A circular pattern is used to start off this purse.

Figure 15   The hairy purse (side view).

The first three rows are tied three times to complete the nine rows of basket weave. The method of decreasing is diagramed in Diagram 76 and may be outlined thus: (row 1) Weave the cords as for a basket weave and tie the square knots as usual, *except* in the four corners. At each corner the four cords are tied in pairs with overhand knots and removed from the pattern as fringe; (row 2) Weave and square-knot as usual; but *after* square-knotting at the corners, remove the four cords as fringe; (row 3) Weave and knot basket weave as usual.

After nine rows, you will have decreased the number of working cords from 160 to 64. Taper each of the four sides to a point in the alternating square knot pattern and finish the tapering edges as you did the purse in Chapter 8.

Thread the four-foot strand of No. 72 cord through the basket weave of row 8 to make a drawstring. Use a piece of wood or leather as a slide for the drawstring and trim the drawstring the length of the fringe.

Thread two 20-foot lengths of No. 72 cord through the basket-weave pattern just below the drawstring, passing the cord from outside in. Bring the four working cords thus formed out the mouth of the purse and tie a strap of reversing square knots (the pattern you used for belt B in Chapter 4). Pass the strap back into the mouth of the purse near point of origin, bringing the cords to the outside through the basket-weave pattern. Tie together in pairs and cut to the length of the fringe. Add leather and a buckle in the middle of the strap (as for a belt) if you want an adjustable strap.

76.

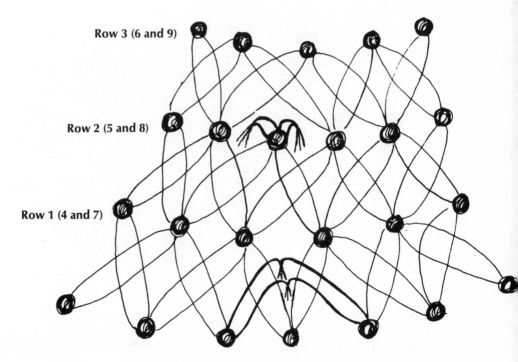

Row 3 (6 and 9)

Row 2 (5 and 8)

Row 1 (4 and 7)

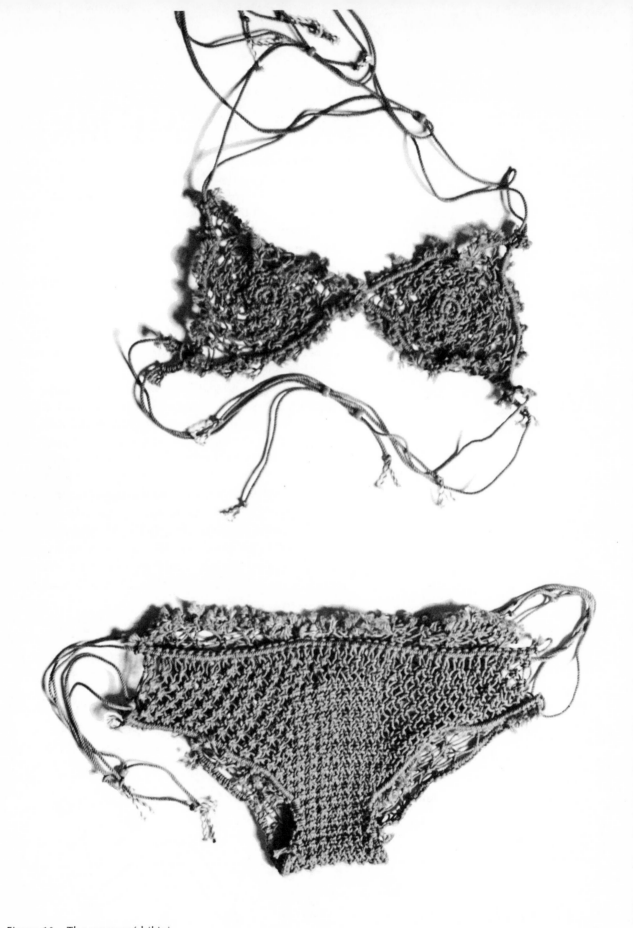

Figure 16   The macramé bikini.

10 A MACRAMÉ BIKINI

Instructions You will need fifty 14-foot lengths of No. 18 or 20 cotton seine twine, 20 feet of No. 42 (in the same color), and seven crow beads (use a contrasting or harmonizing color). A tying board will be used. The directions given here are for a size 7 to 9 suit.

Top Cut ten 14-foot lengths into quarters so that you have 40 cords, 20 for each cup. Tie the basic circle used for the hat in Chapter 7 to produce 20 working cords. Tie two rows of alternating square knots, adjusting the tension so that the pattern gently curves to fit the body. Add the remaining 10 cords and continue to tie square knots until cup is the desired size and shape. Repeat for the second cup.

To finish the top, cut two lengths of No. 42 cord, each about 40 inches long. One will form the horizontal strap encircling the chest, and the other will fit around the neck. Two 10-inch lengths of No. 42 cord will form the sides of the roughly triangular cups. The exact order of attachment of the working cords to the No. 42 edge cords will vary with the suit: one good arrangement is shown in Diagram 77. In attaching the cords to the edge, use the clove hitch followed by a half hitch and fill in with lark's head knots so that the edge cord is covered by the working cords. Tie overhand knots in the working cords and trim close (Diagrams 77 and 78).

The side pieces of No. 42 cord are joined to the neck and back straps by square-knotting short lengths of last working cords (if there is not enough working cord left, you can add on a short piece of discarded cord) over the two cords to be joined for about ¾ inch and then cutting off the leftover side cord (see Diagram 77).

77.   **Cut off side cord after square-knotting**

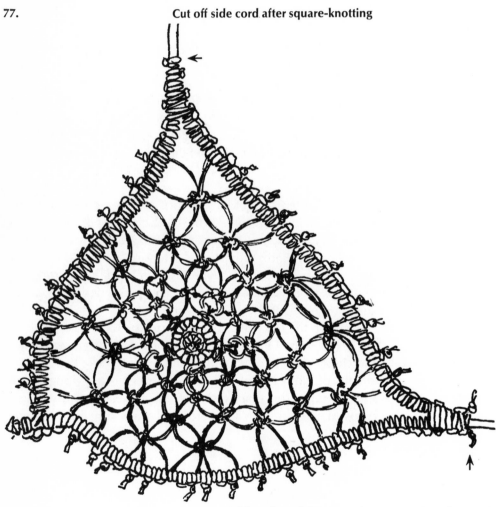

Add cords and tie square knots over the edge cords

78.

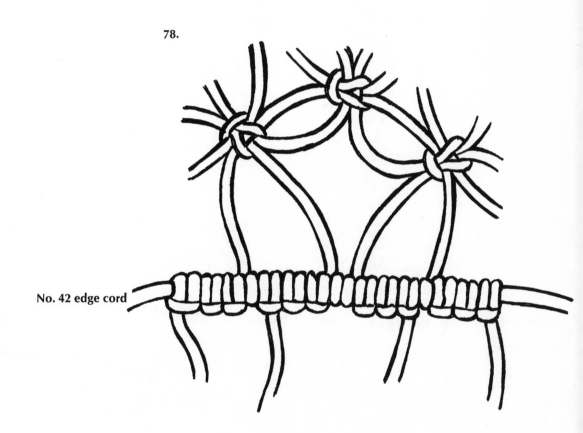

No. 42 edge cord

Thread the neck and back straps through crow beads. This permits the suit to be put on and adjusted simply by pulling on the ends of the strap cords to tighten the straps (Diagram 79).

79.

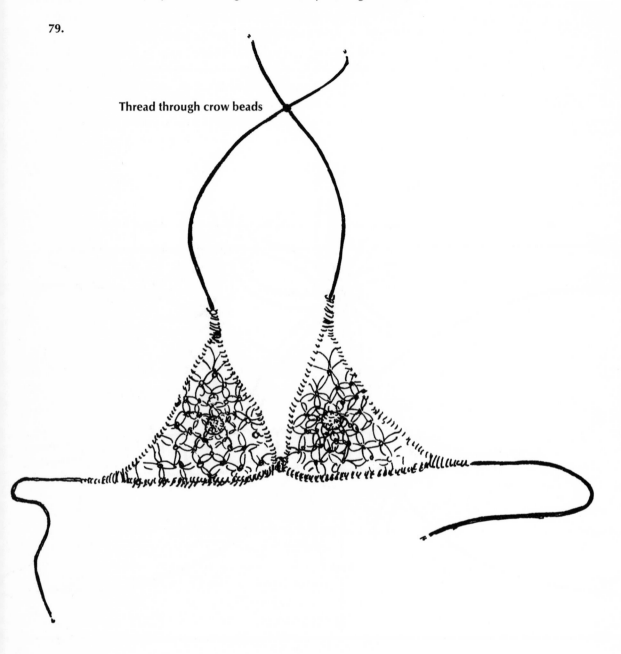

Thread through crow beads

Bottom   Use a tying board laid out as in Diagram 80. Start by fastening a horizontal carrier cord of No. 42 cord for the top front. Hitch on twelve 14-foot-long cords in the center, alternating them with a spacer cord as you did for the purse front in Chapter 8. Add twelve 7-foot cords, also separated by the spacer cord, on each side of the center section. Tie a row of square knots ½ inch below the carrier cord, followed by two rows of alternating square knots about ⅜ inch apart. So that the wearer won't be arrested at the beach, begin working the center section of the suit in a more tightly knotted alternating square knot pattern. Since the spaces between rows in this

80.

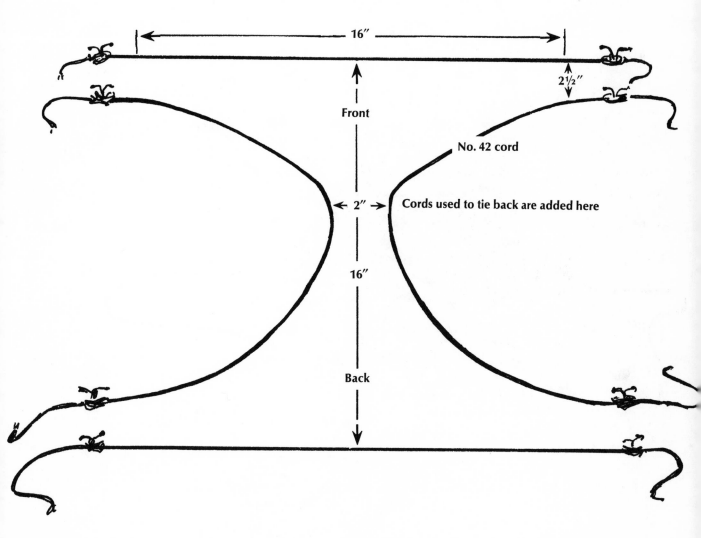

16"

2½"

Front

No. 42 cord

← 2" →   **Cords used to tie back are added here**

16"

Back

center section will be about half the distance between rows of the adjacent open pattern, tie the pattern illustrated in Diagram 81 and gradually widen this dense portion as you continue down the piece.

When the side of the suit is 2½ to 3 inches deep, begin to taper the lower edge along the lines indicated in Diagram 80. Taper the pattern until you are working with the central 24 cords. Use two lengths of No. 42 cord about 30 inches long for the lower edges of the suit, and hitch the working cords over them in usual fashion. Using the central 24 cords, continue the tightly tied pattern through the crotch. The last front working cord to be hitched over the edge cord on either side is continued through the crotch and tied in lark's heads over the carrier cord, securing the edges of the pattern (Diagram 82).

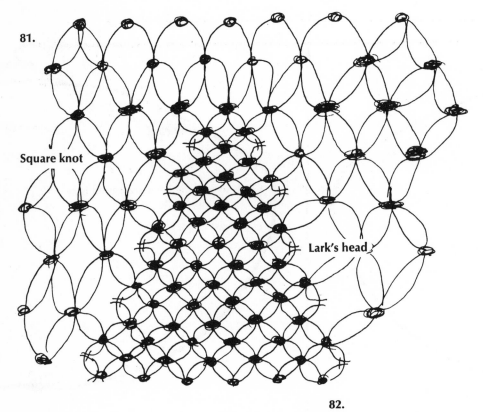

81.

Square knot

Lark's head

82.

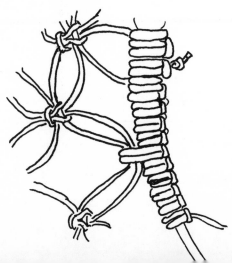

When the crotch is long enough, begin to widen the piece by adding more 7-foot lengths of cord along the edge cords (see Diagram 80). These added cords are used to tie an alternating square knot pattern in a density determined by the wearer's modesty. See Figure 17 for one way to finish the back section of the suit.

Finish the bottom by clove-hitching the working cords over the second horizontal carrier cord forming the upper border of the suit back. Tie and trim the cords.

Assemble the suit by threading the No. 42 cords through crow beads as in Diagram 83.

83.   Assembling the bikini bottom

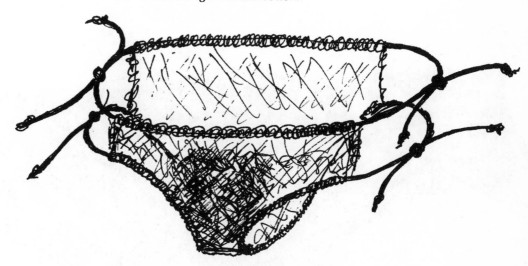

Figure 17   The macramé bikini, front and back.

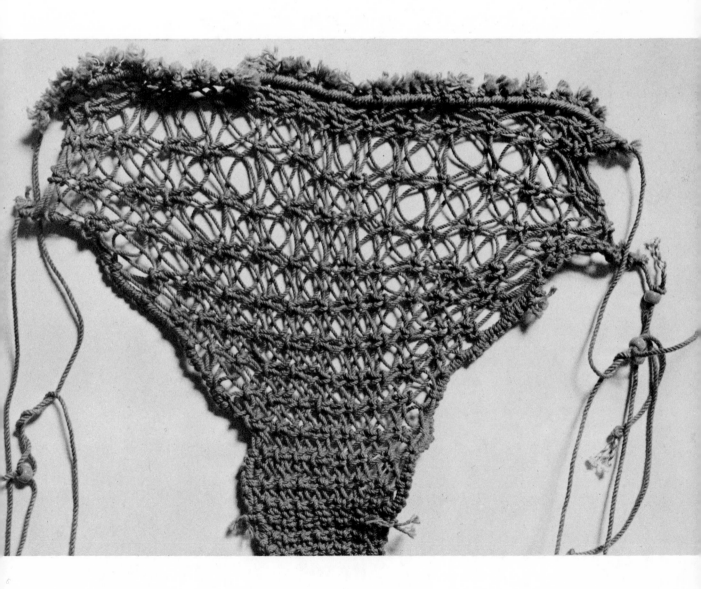

11 MACRAMÉ VESTS
(WAISTCOATS)

Most vests (waistcoats) can be tied with 1½ to 2 pounds of No. 42 cotton seine twine in standard lengths of 14 feet. For exceptionally close or longer patterns, use proportionately longer cord. No. 42 twine is easily threaded through crow beads, and two cords can be threaded through one bead with practice. On the beaded styles crow beads and tile beads are used. I have made a vest with No. 48 nylon and find it only slightly more difficult to use than cotton.

The secret of tying a vest (waistcoast) is the tying board: once you allocate space on the board, you have only to fill it in with designs of your liking. Begin according to Diagram 84.

84.

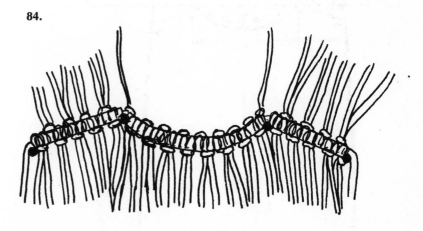

Figure 18   Back of a V-necked vest.

There are two basic styles which Ellen and I tie. The first to be developed was a short model, open in the front, which requires somewhat precise fitting. Later, Ellen devised a V-neck pattern which fits over the head and ties down the sides. This pattern is less closely fitted and sized small, medium, or large, it will fit most people.

The two basic tying boards we use are illustrated in Diagrams 85 and 86.

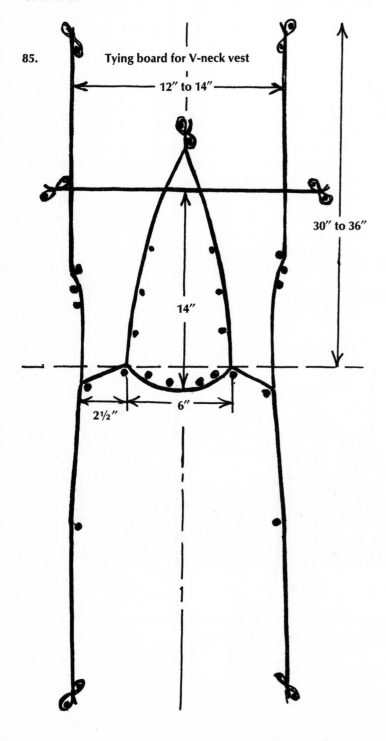

85.   **Tying board for V-neck vest**

12" to 14"

30" to 36"

14"

2½"

6"

86.

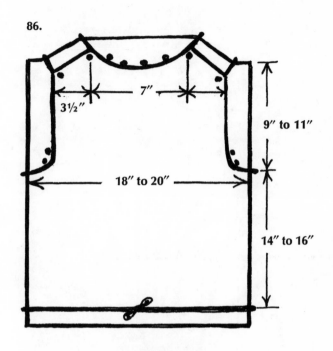

Front and back views of tying board for regular vest

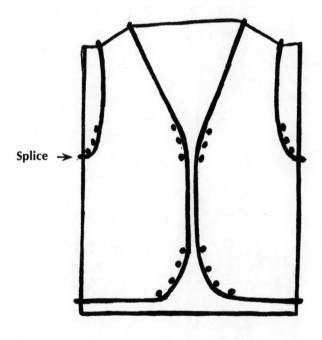

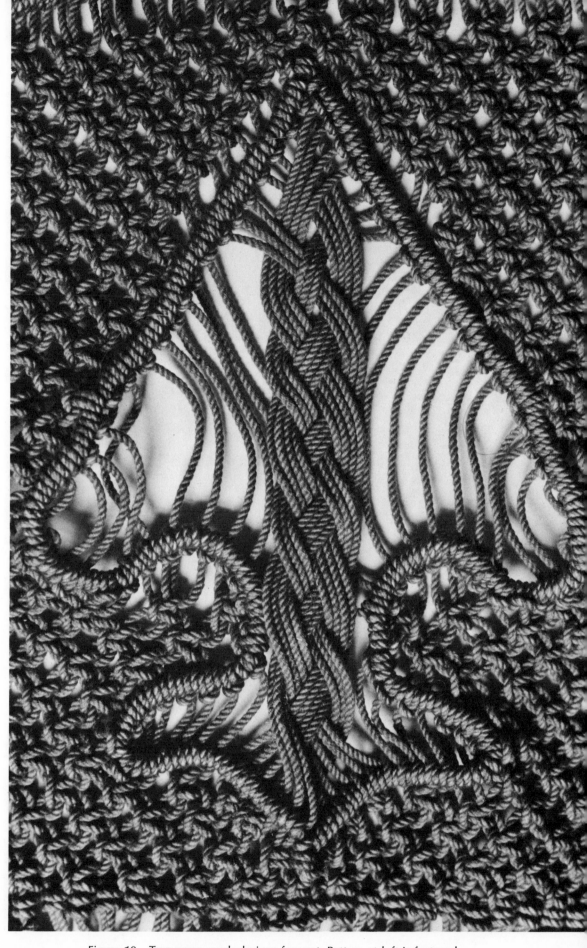

Figure 19   Two open-work designs for vest. Pattern at left is featured
on vest in Figure 18.

Figure 20 More patterns for the macramé vest.

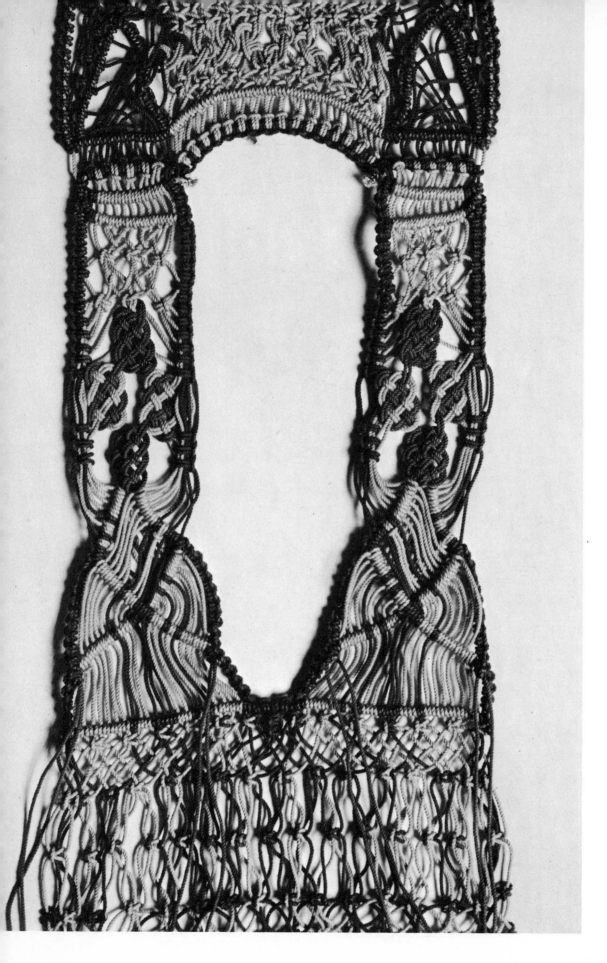

Figure 21   Top view of a macramé vest, showing shoulder pattern.

12 SOME NOTES

The techniques you have learned are applicable to any macramé piece. The designing of a vest back, for example, is not very different from laying out a wall hanging. If you wish—and I hope you don't—you could even make a placemat.

There are many fancy knots which we haven't even mentioned. Most ornamental knots are tied by following a diagram, and unless you use them a lot, it is hardly necessary to be able to tie them from memory. You can look them up as you need them. To get you started, here are three ornamental knots which we usually tie with doubled cord laid flat. Ornamental knots and braids are both really interlocking knots and are stabilized by interweaving.

If you wish a reference book on macramé, I would suggest the *Encyclopedia of Knots and Fancy Rope Work* (4th Ed.) by Raoul Graumont and John Hensel, published by the Cornell Maritime Press. *Macramé* by Virginia Harvey, published by Van Nostrand Reinhold, is also a good reference.

87. Josephine knot

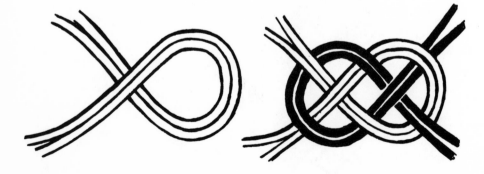

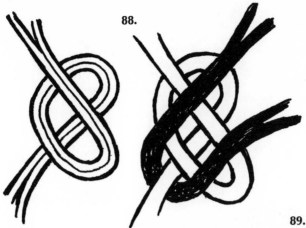

88.

89. Lupé knot

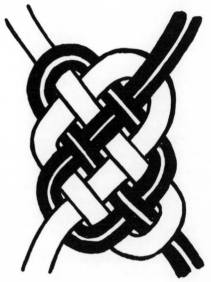

90. Fancy braiding

LIST OF SUPPLIERS

Many suppliers in the eastern part of the United States carry cord instead of seine twine. Cable cord is made from coarser yarn than seine twine and is more loosely twisted, but it may be substituted for cotton seine twine if necessary. Because of the larger yarn and the softer twist, cable cord of a certain number will be larger than cotton seine twine of the same number, so we have provided a table showing the sizes of cable cord to substitute for the sizes of cotton seine twine recommended in the text.

	Cotton seine twine	Cable cord
Size	24	18
	42	24
	72	48

United States

National Mail-Order Houses

Craft Yarns of Rhode Island, P.O. Box 385, Pawtucket, R.I. 02862, has cotton and nylon seine twine, macramé cord, various ornamental braided cords.

Tandy Leather Company, Inc./American Handicrafts Company, Inc., 20 West 14th Street and 384 Fifth Avenue, New York City, has over 140 other retail stores nationwide, with varied supplies of macramé material. Free literature on macramé supplies may be obtained by writing Tandy Leather Company, Inc., Box 791, Fort Worth, Texas 76101

Retail Stores (Also Mail-Order)

The Works, 319 South Street, Philadelphia, Pa. 19147, has cotton and nylon seine twine, dyed and undyed; ceramic beads.

J. E. Fricke, 40 North Front Street, Philadelphia, Pa. 19106, has cable cord, jute twine, linen, sisal, and hemp twines and ropes.

Elisha Weber and Son, 126 South Front Street, Philadelphia, Pa. 19106, has marine hardware—brass and bronze rings, snaps, shackles, thimbles, and other small hardware items useful for belts and hangings.

Seaboard Twine and Cordage Co., 49 Murray Street, New York, N.Y. 10007, has cotton and nylon seine twine in all sizes, braided nylon seine twine, cable cord, macramé cord, jute twine.

Joseph M. Hart, 16 Reade Street, New York, N.Y. 10007, has leather-working tools and supplies, brass rings and buckles.

La Nasa Hardware Co., 1027 Decatur Street, New Orleans, La. 70116, has cotton and nylon seine twine in all sizes, many twisted and braided cords and ropes in cotton and nylon.

The Sun Shop, 7722 Maple Street, New Orleans, La. 70118, has cotton and nylon seine twine, dyed and undyed; jute twine, macramé cord, rings, buckles, hemostats, bells, all types of glass and ceramic beads suitable for macramé.

United Kingdom

C & F Handicraft Suppliers, 346 Stag Lane, Kingsbury, London, NW9

Dryads, Northgates, Leicester

The Needlewoman, 146 Regent Street, London W1